T0129260

# RACISM: A GLOBAL PROBLEM

JOSEPH GODSON AMAMOO

authorHOUSE®

AuthorHouse™ UK
1663 Liberty Drive
Bloomington, IN 47403 USA
www.authorhouse.co.uk
Phone: 0800.197.4150

Published by AuthorHouse  04/30/2016

ISBN: 978-1-5049-9518-4 (sc)
ISBN: 978-1-5049-9519-1 (hc)
ISBN: 978-1-5049-9533-7 (e)

*This book is dedicated to all men and women of all races who have made a contribution however large or small towards the elimination of racism in the world.*

# Contents

# PREFACE

The year 1945 witnessed the defeat of Fascism at the end of the Second World War. This was followed by the collapse of Communism in 1989-1990. Finally in 1994 came the demise of Apartheid in South Africa. Thus within a period of just a few years short of fifty, three major ideologies, which had caused the deaths of millions of people of all races, had been expunged from the world. The tragedies unfolded by these three obnoxious ideologies have one major thing in common.

White people - that is, people of European origin or extraction, initiated each and every one of them. Also white people put them all into effect, although their institutionalization and promotion involved the deaths (on a large scale) of many non-Europeans, who became victims of programs and activities that they had no hand in bringing into reality.

As the twenty-first century progresses, the next global ideology that will have to be confronted and defeated is Racism. This ideology that white people or people of European origin or ancestry are superior to non-Europeans has been with the world since the fifteenth century when Europeans began to interact with people in Asia and Africa on a large scale. And over the centuries it has become ingrained in the lives of many white people in Europe and the Americas.

In this work I endeavor to outline the harm and hurt that racism has done and is doing to nonwhite people and also the probable baneful results and repercussions that the continued practice of racism will produce on white people. Although in theory and indeed in practice, but on a very limited scale, racism by nonwhites against white people does occur. But generally racism is invariably understood as discriminatory practices and programs against Asians and Africans and people of African descent.

The reason is that to date nonwhite people have not been in a position to practice racism against white people. For dislike or discrimination by black people, without the power to make it effective, is futile and meaningless. But as is shown in this work with the independence and economic development of many Asian and African nations, the situation is rapidly changing where racism against white people is becoming a reality. And it is my firm conviction that this situation can easily be avoided if Europeans and people of European origin or ancestry cooperate towards the noble end of ending racism altogether.

The sources for my work are three fold. First there are my own personal experiences in Europe and America, the two, major bastions of racism. Secondly, the experiences and stories of Asians and Africans (and African Americans), who have experienced racism firsthand. And thirdly, books, stories and articles about racism that I have read in the course of my life. My work is not meant as an academic treatise but as a heart-felt and mindful reflection on a major issue of global significance that if not addressed will quickly lead to further unnecessary incidents of violence and conflict in many parts of the world. I maintain that such conflicts are avoidable and that if they cause the deaths or injuries or suffering of even only a few people, there is no reason or justification why this should happen.

A superficial reading of this book may give the impression that it is racist. Far from it! What I am merely trying to do is to make a modest contribution to inter-racial harmony and draw the urgent attention of white people worldwide, including colleagues and friends, that not only is it right that the burden of racism is lifted off their shoulders but also that the continued practice and propagation of this evil and dangerous idea or program will inexorably have consequences and repercussions on their children and grandchildren. No sane person would want this to happen. I certainly don't.

If this book does nothing more than generate a healthy honest and open debate on racism and why white people should not encourage it in any shape or form, then it would have served a useful purpose, however small. I take this opportunity to thank all those people, European, Asian, American and African, who in one way or another have helped me over the years to find a healthy understanding of racism and its negative and dangerous effects both short and long term on both black and white people. Long live inter-racial harmony and peaceful coexistence.

I'm happy to place on record here my immense gratitude to Diana Mary Sitek of Minneapolis, Minn USA, who by editing this work and making considerable corrections and suggestions enormously improved the book, however any errors or mistakes still inherent in the book are my own responsibility. Also my good friend, Kojo Marfo of London, England has given considerable assistance in typing this work, making suggestions here and there. I thank him from the bottom of my heart.

The publisher's production team led by Kim Cavannah has done a superb job in the production of this book and I cannot thank them enough.

To Breid my wife for over fifty three years, who has assisted me in various ways, including acting as the sounding board for many of my ideas, I extend my limitless and profound gratitude. Her own bold and principled stand against racism over a period of sixty years is outstanding.

Signed: JOSEPH GODSON AMAMOO

# WHAT IS RACISM?

Of all the definitions of racism I find that of the world renowned encyclopedia, Wikipedia, the best. It defines Racism as "Ideologies centered around the concept of race." The term is usually understood as discrimination and a body of discriminatory practices based on the belief that certain races are superior to others." Although this concept or belief can apply to all races to the extent that racism is only meaningful if it is buttressed by political, military or economic power, the term has certainly over the past few decades come to mean discrimination by white people against nonwhite people.

In other words, although in theory nonwhites can also practice racism, until the middle of the twentieth century they have not been in the political position to do so. It means that Africans and Asians and other peoples of non-European origin or extraction have not been able to indulge in racism, even if they wanted to or have a propensity to so do.

Racism exists in most countries but particularly in the Americas and Europe. Although in Europe there is racism against the Romany people, sometimes known as Gypsies, generally and globally such forms of racism are limited to specific regions. In any case, to the extent that many Romany people look European or white, they do not tend to suffer racial discrimination as Africans and Asians do. I recall chatting with a white English man in a Kentish town in

England several years ago, not knowing that he was of the Romany race until he so identified himself.

In other words people who are not easily and physically identified or recognizable as nonwhite are not victims of racism to the same degree and extent as Africans and Asians. That the physical and visible dimension of racism is an integral aspect of the phenomenon is demonstrated by the fact that people who look white are not so discriminated against until they speak or show in one way or another that they are not of the race of the person addressing them.

For example, I have known cases of white English men who are strongly against Romany people (Gypsies)and without knowing had interacted in a very friendly manner with them until they learnt that they were Romany people. Also, at the height of racism in both the United States of America and apartheid South Africa, some people, who as a result of their biracial origin or were extreme albinos, and looked white, tried to pass themselves off as white. Whilst some succeeded, others failed to do so.

In this work I use the term white as generally understood all over the world. This is, strictly speaking, incorrect terminology. For as George Bernard Shaw, the celebrated British writer, said: "We are pink, not white", a fact which even the most rabid proponent of white supremacy will find it difficult to deny, if evaluating the skin color of people of European ancestry or origins.

The concept of racial superiority was strengthened in Europe in the nineteenth century as propounded by fake sciences such as Phrenology, making people believe that the shape of the skull reflected the character, or intelligence, of a person. This misconception caused white people to believe black people are inferior to white people intellectually, culturally and morally. Off course, with the evaluation or assessment being done by white people the results were predictable!

Racism reached its apogee from 1933 when the Nazis came to power in Germany. From then on through the Nuremberg Laws and other laws ruthlessly enforced by ardent agents of the regime, racism became part and parcel of the Nazi dictatorship. Its spread by military force in the countries occupied by the conquering Nazi forces led to the extermination of six million Jews and millions of others including Gypsies, the mentally and physically handicapped and homosexuals. For under the Nazi doctrine, they were inferior and must be exterminated.

The horrendous consequences for the whole world of not nipping in the bud such an evil and dangerous ideology were not only the massive destruction of cities and towns and other infrastructure but more importantly the deaths of over forty two million people of all races, twenty four million of whom were Russians or citizens of the Soviet Union, defunct since 1992.

The carnage resulting from the Second World War (1939—1945) plus the cataclysmic events leading up to the war demonstrate that it is in the enlightened self-interest of all people, irrespective of race or skin color, to fight racism and ensure its immediate elimination from the whole world. For like a cancerous tumor, if not destroyed early or in time, any subsequent palliative or curative intervention becomes more difficult and more costly.

The spread of fascism in Portugal, Spain and Italy from the early 1930's also led to the growth of racism in these countries. However, as there were practically no black people in these countries, the racism virulent as it was operated in the African and Asian colonies of Italy, Spain and Portugal.

Evidence that racism has a major economic component is provided by the discernible trend that peoples or races who had previously been marginalized or discriminated against by white people have, on becoming economically and industrially developed and advanced, ceased to be victims of discrimination.

A classic case is that of Japan. As a non-European nation it was the victim of racism in diverse ways in the nineteenth and twentieth centuries. By the 1970s its economic power had become phenomenally great. It had developed to become the largest economic power in the whole world, surpassed by only the USA. Quietly and suddenly, the racism disappeared. Indeed, the reverse process appears to be progressing, with more and more nations and peoples, not only in Europe but elsewhere, lauding Japanese way of life, manufactured goods and expertise. If one considers the fact that Japan's population is only 128 million, then it is astonishing how it was able to maintain its position as the second largest economy in the world till 2010, when it was overtaken by China, with a population of 1.3 billion, about ten times that of Japan. The GDP for Japan at $5.5 trillion as at 2010 compares with that for China at $5.9 trillion. This means that the second and third largest economies in the whole world now are Asian. that is, non-European. This fact thus further demolishes one of the fundamental bases of racism.

Not only is racism a vicious and dangerous ideology with no scientific or rational basis whatsoever but it is also counter-productive. However, if the racists are factually right then they owe the enlightened, non-racist people in the world the explanation why two Asian countries should hold the economic positions that they hold now, especially as the industrial revolution started in Europe, specifically in the United Kingdom in the nineteenth century. And it was several decades before it reached these countries aforementioned. Naturally, immense and gargantuan challenges, hurdles and obstacles had to be faced and overcome as those who had industrialized their economies were not at all keen to assist others to do likewise. Considering that the population of Japan is 128 million against 320 million for the USA then the achievements of Japan become even more breathtaking and outstanding.

This rapid economic and industrial advancement and progress go to explain the disappearance of racism against the Japanese. It also goes to buttress the fact that racism, stripped of the economic power and the power from the military/industrial complex underpinning it, becomes a hollow ideology, destined to collapse in the near future.

The racists are wrong and have for centuries been peddling self-serving ideologies and promoting activities which have gone unchallenged because they were in the political and military positions to enforce their will and views on those whom they deemed or classified as racially inferior to themselves.

It follows therefore that as the intricate network of coercive force dwindles or disappears, the ideologies and practices associated with it will collapse. And it is my considered opinion that it is absolutely unnecessary that thousands of people have to die or suffer before the inevitable end of racism. Even the death or suffering of one person, physical or psychological, because of his/her race, is in my view completely unjustified and devoid of any sound arguments on grounds of necessity.

Where we cannot see the writing on the wall, metaphorically speaking, then there is an excuse for aberrant behavior. But where, with a modicum of intelligence, foresight and realism, one can see the writing clearly on the wall, then rationally there is no excuse whatsoever for perpetuating a system, which is not only immoral and cruel but ultimately can and will damage enormously those who promote it.

# CHAPTER 2

# TYPES OF RACISM

The evil ideology manifests itself in various forms but generally as discrimination against one set of people by another group on grounds of their race, identified as skin color. Outlined below are a few classic and well-known classifications of racism

INTERNAL RACISM: This is demonstrated by discrimination against a section of the national population, usually a minority by the majority, because of the physical appearance of the minority. Invariably the discrimination is based on clearly visible identity such as skin color.

Take for instance the United Kingdom with which I am modestly familiar, having spent the greater part of my adult life studying, living and working there. Although racism has gone down considerably and is nowhere near in the state it was when I arrived in the country in September 1957, still even now in the second decade of the twenty first century, it is far easier for a white person with inferior qualifications to get a job or financial assistance than a nonwhite person. This is irrespective of the fact that both persons were born in the country and thus theoretically and legally are equal citizens, entitled to the same rights, privileges and subject to the same legal and national obligations. Even a person newly arrived in the United Kingdom from Eastern Europe, not a British-born citizen and speaking barely passable English stands a better chance of getting a job than a British born Asian or African or Afro Caribbean.

Whilst recently shopping in North London, I have talked with some Africans or Asians working as security men or as shop assistants. In each and every case they told me that although they held degrees and in some cases, master's degrees from British universities, they could not get suitable jobs and had to accept their current positions of about 7.50 pounds sterling per hour,(about 11 dollars) standing for very long, boring hours. Very distressing for me was the fact that their parents had to make immense financial sacrifices for them to get those qualifications. Having been out of the job market or house hunting for many years and rather naively believing that such situations no longer existed, I was very upset that the old racism that I knew of in my student days long ago was still alive and thriving. Admittedly it is not as overt as before and not as virulent, but nevertheless still in existence.

Although I have not conducted any surveys in other European countries, talking with nonwhite people from Asia and Africa, I have concluded that the situation is no different in those countries. If anything at all, the racism in the United Kingdom is less compared with elsewhere in Europe and South America.

In the United Kingdom, whilst indeed Asian and Africans suffer from racism, it is noteworthy that generally the Asians have resolved the problems and the challenges that they face by favoring self-employment more than has been achieved by Africans or people of African descent.

Clear evidence of this achievement and trend is their ownership or control of thousands of small corner shops, pharmacies and family run post offices in Britain. By being prepared to put in very long hours daily, (often as long as twelve hours), for six days a week they have circumvented racism or greatly minimized its deleterious effects. This is a field of economic activity which until the arrival of the East African Asians in the early 1970's was predominantly controlled by indigenous white people.

On the other hand, British born Afro-Caribbeans and Africans tend to gravitate to employment in local government and other public services, such as the Civil service, Education, Royal Mail, London Transport, Railways and the National Health Service. Why? Because many of the Afro-Caribbean and other identifiable minorities, devoid of the needed capital to go into business, find the public services and other semi-state bodies less racist and more welcoming. For these major employers being state or semi–state groupings are more sensitive to the need for them to be seen to be responding to the anti-racism laws passed by Parliament.

In the private sector, although subject to the same laws against racism as the non-private sector, to the extent that employers, large or small, come from the same society as the rest of the population, it is rational to expect that their attitudes to racism reflect those of the general society. And indeed this is the case.

Even in the fields of entertainment, fashion and the liberal arts, where people are deemed to be forward looking and progressive, generally the same ugly head of racism rears itself. Thus in recent years, a few prominent black icons in these fields, who have broken the glass ceiling and can therefore afford to complain in public, have bemoaned the unfair, racist practices that young, up and coming black people, with great potential still in the twenty first century have to endure.

Naomi Campbell, the British born, international super-model and Lenny Henry, the well-known British comedian and actor may be mentioned here. There are a few others who have gone public. But I daresay there must be hundreds of other prominent and successful black men and women who share the same concerns as Naomi Campbell and Lenny Henry but who find that the stakes are too high in going public and that career-wise, silence is the best option.

There must be millions of white people who accept and believe that racism is wrong, immoral and unjustified but do nothing about it, although they are not racists themselves. Why? Because firstly, they would not want to be ridiculed or ostracized by their compatriots. Secondly, being economic, political or social beneficiaries of the vile inhuman system, for them to work against the system or promote its demise is in effect like undertaking the destruction of the very system that they are benefitting from enormously. And this is a very tall order for many ordinary human beings, who are devoid of saintly qualities. To put it rather insensitively, it is like asking cigarette manufacturers to actively join in the campaign against smoking. For a lukewarm or negative support from them does not mean or should not be taken to mean or suggest that all the manufacturers and those actively and robustly associated in the trade promoting smoking, individually or collectively are unaware or unmindful of the health dangers and hazards posed by smoking.

Realistically, one cannot in all fairness criticize the thousands of successful and wealthy black people in various walks of life, particularly in entertainment, broadcasting, fashion, music and sports who choose to keep quiet about racism. For with all the command and control positions, bar a tiny few, in Europe and the Americas held by white people, it becomes rather risky and unwise to go public with one's concerns, however justified. Charles Darwin's Theory of the Survival of the Fittest underpins the muted approach of many people towards blatant racism, even when they feel the strong urge to vent their opinions.

Furthermore, the history of the world consistently demonstrates that those who have been in the forefront of major political or social changes in their countries have paid a very high price for their idealism and altruism.

Such outstanding men and women, right at the time of their advocacy and campaigning, although subsequently hailed and revered as national heroes, were not spared savage public ridicule and sometimes even violent assaults. The Suffragette Movement in the United Kingdom in the early twentieth century is a case in point. Looking back, it is very difficult to understand how and why mature, intelligent human beings in Britain could rationally make a case for not allowing women to vote because they were women per se. No compelling and irrefutable evidence was ever produced to support the idea or concept of the inferiority of females. It was all a hodgepodge of prejudice, bigotry and ignorance masquerading as enlightenment. That powerful religious leaders joined in the mass opposition to women's rights demonstrates that despite their special and privileged positions as spiritual leaders of their people, they were also subject to the prevailing prejudices, customs and traditions of their time.

Internal Racism may manifest itself as institutional racism. That is, where a body or group has the official policy of descrimination against a visble racial minority. However in all countries, institutional racism has dissapeared in its overt form as national laws have been effected against it but conditions can be so created that the racism is not overt but covert: For example: To join a police force or military, physical and academic conditions are such that it's hardly possible for a certain minority.

The opposition to granting women the vote is made even more untenable on grounds of democracy. For by denying them the vote, as there are slightly more females than males in the United Kingdom and in most countries it means in effect the denial of the vote by the minority against the majority. And this obviously is not democratic.

As the success of the suffragettes in the United Kingdom has shown, any ideology or political program that is underpinned by coercive force or the threat of force, but is devoid of a sound, moral basis is destined to fail, even if initially it succeeds for some time, perhaps even decades or centuries. It follows by this line of reasoning that racism, however long it survives, is ultimately destined for the dustbin of social and political history. And it is really a matter of grave concern that many Europeans and people of European descent cannot see or refuse to see the palpable, unmistakable trend of world history.

EXTERNAL RACISM: By this I mean racial discrimination based on the fact that the victim is from another race as identified by his skin color. Thus in Europe and the Americas once a person looks darkish in complexion or has the features usually associated with peoples from the Middle East, Africa or Asia, he/she risks being discriminated against. This is irrespective of the probability that he/she is a true born citizen of the particular country. Once again, it is corroborative evidence that racism is based predominantly on physical features, especially skin color. This form of racism was particularly active in the European colonies in Asia, Africa, the Middle East, South America and the Caribbean islands. As such as the countries in the aforementioned areas became independent from colonial rule, the racism died out.

# CHAPTER 3

# HISTORICAL BACKGROUND

From the sixteenth to the middle of the twentieth century practically all countries in Asia; the Middle East and Africa were colonies of the major European countries, such as Britain; France; Germany; Italy; the Netherlands; Belgium; Portugal and Spain. Where those countries were not direct colonies, they were under the sphere of influence of the major powers, as Protectorates, with virtually little difference from the status of a colony. It should be noted here that Germany and Italy lost their colonies after the end of the First World War.

However, in all the countries under European control racism was established as government policy. Thus the upper echelons of the civil service were exclusively for whites and the handful of indigenous people trained in universities of the colonial masters. The latter still could not get the same jobs as their white counterparts with the same qualifications. Indeed it was sensational news when during the Second World War two Ghanaian born Oxford University graduates were appointed District Commissioners (representatives of the British colonial administration). For until then no black person had ever been appointed. Whatever their qualifications, to the extent that they were not European or looked European, they were excluded. The question of qualifications did not come into any consideration to appoint them. Highly educated indigenous people with even better qualifications than their white counterparts were told in the colonial

Gold Coast (Ghana since independence in March 1957) that they had the qualifications but not the relevant experience. And those who had risen through the ranks in the civil service were told that yes, they had the relevant experience but lacked the appropriate qualifications. Yet young British Oxbridge graduates fresh from university were being appointed, donning the official white helmet and wearing the spotlessly white uniform, the ensemble that constituted their power and authority. Of course the usual armed black police escort was ever present.

However inhuman racism was in the British colonies, it pales into insignificance compared with the situation in the other European colonies in Africa. For example, by the time the British granted independence to Ghana in 1957, there were a few British trained military officers with the ranks of major and captain. But by the time the Belgians left the Congo in 1963 after a longer period than the British had been in charge of the Gold Coast, the highest ranking military person was a mere sergeant.

Equally disturbing, and emphasizing the severity and intensity of the racism in the Congo, readers may note that whilst by 1957 there were, in Ghana, many indigenous doctors and lawyers trained in British universities, in the Congo the highest educated local person was a Roman Catholic priest. There were no doctors, lawyers, engineers, architects or other professionals. Yet there is no evidence whatsoever that the people in the Congo were less intelligent or less capable than those in the Gold Coast or Nigeria. The differences in development and achievements alluded to between the two groups of Africans in sub-Saharan Africa were the results of two clearly defined and implemented policies of racism.

The deleterious effects of racism in the British and Belgian colonies were replicated in the other colonies controlled by the other European powers like France, Spain, Portugal, and Italy.

By the time of independence from colonial rule by all the countries in Africa, the institutions which were established to prop and maintain racism had become endemic and deep seated. This phenomenon is not all that surprising, given that the various colonial periods lasted in some cases more than a century.

In each instance, the viciousness and intensity of the racism were directly proportional to the numbers of Europeans in the particular African country. Thus in West Africa, where there were very few white people, either as employees or self-employed, the racism was rather benign and bearable for the vast majority of the local people. Whilst in those countries which because of the equable weather conditions and terrain, white settlement in considerable numbers were possible, the racism was intense and brutal.

That the perpetrators of the racism were Christians or claimed so to be, made no blind difference to their palpably unchristian behavior and activities. Thus the people in East Africa and Southern Africa suffered far more from racism than West Africa. Ironically this was the price that they had to pay for providing an ideal environmental and climatic conditions for European settlement.

With the ending of colonialism in Africa in the mid nineteen sixties, racism against indigenous Africans suffered a mortal blow. Admittedly it did not disappear completely overnight. For how realistically could a system that had existed and thrived for at least a couple of centuries just suddenly be erased? But with the military, political and economic underpinning removed, the ideology became stripped of the oxygen that it needed to survive.

Furthermore, with political power (and with it judicial power) now in the hands of indigenous Africans it became rather foolhardy and unwise for any European or white person to talk or behave in any way or manner that might be construed or viewed as racist by the new rulers or their fellow compatriots.

The sudden changes in white attitudes in Africa and Asia explain why however racist a white man may be in Europe or America, once he sets foot on the soil of Africa or Asia, either on business or pleasure or for whatever purpose, he quickly and instinctively realizes that for his own good he has to bottle his racism and wait to give vent to it when he returns home. For to do otherwise would be far too risky and rather stupid!

The fact that a white person who may be a virulent racist at home can under certain environmental conditions suppress his racism and talk and behave without a trace of racism goes to show, in my humble view, that racism is not genetic. Any person, however rabidly racist, can be deprogrammed, especially if his own self-interest, livelihood or welfare is at stake, at the given time and place.

So in effect what I term 'external racism', bad and evil as it is, can easily be eradicated or terminated. The process need not and does not deserve to be violent. All that is needed is to ensure a transfer of political power from the tiny minority group practicing racism to the visible majority who are the victims of racism.

As demonstrated by events in the Republic of South Africa since the end of apartheid in 1994 it is feasible for even white people who have been steeped in violent racism for several decades to adopt and develop new and healthy social and political attitudes that enhance the welfare and progress of not only the former victims of racism but also the people who had for centuries perpetuated the vicious and brutal system.

Since the advent of democratic majority rule in South Africa, not based on skin color or race but on the results of free, fair and transparent nation elections, there have been very rare cases of white people prosecuted for racism. That there are still a tiny minority of white diehards who yearn and hanker after 'the good old days of apartheid' must not be at all surprising. After all, in a population of over five million they all cannot be expected to think and behave alike. So in the circumstances it is indeed remarkable how smoothly and peacefully the white people in South Africa have adjusted to and accepted the political and social changes that have overwhelmed them in a matter of a few years. Considering that the psychological and social impacts of the changes must have been dramatic, one cannot but admire their robust spirit of resilience and realism.

The relatively good interracial relations between the predominantly black African majority population in South Africa and their compatriots of European extraction or descent, constituting about five percent of the national population indicates that indeed racism can be overcome, however ingrained.

The problem as evidenced in Asia and Africa during the periods of the struggles for independence from colonial rule has been with the generation of white people who had known and enjoyed the huge benefits accruing from racism and colonialism and then had to face the reality of being stripped of their privileges and power. Quite rightly, post-apartheid white people in South Africa have learnt that peaceful coexistence between them and the black majority, devoid of racism, is the best option.

Of course, there have been a very few people of European origin who have left the country rather than live under black majority rule. Thus it is estimated (Wikipedia, 2014) that since end of apartheid 800,000 have left the country, although some have returned. But the overwhelming majority of them have not followed the few who have left, mostly for Australia, South America and Western Europe. Each person or family had to choose whether to stay put and enjoy their relatively comfortable lives but without the benefits bestowed by racism or uproot themselves and relocate to new countries where the vast majority of the population were of the same race as themselves. It may be noted that their new countries are all places where although racism is officially illegal is nevertheless tolerated by the generality of the population.

So in effect, assuming that the new immigrants carry to their new lands the same racist attitudes and behaviors that they had in South Africa, it would mean that they had advanced the internal racism in their new countries. In other words external racism has metamorphosed into internal racism. And it is arguable whether such an outcome would be good and beneficial to their new adopted home countries.

As external racism is intertwined with colonial rule in Asia, the Middle East, Asia-Pacific and Africa, the independence of all the countries in those regions have led to the end of racism in those regions.

# CHAPTER 4

# THE COMPARISONS FROM CRADLE TO THE GRAVE

The main concept of racism is based on the view that certain races or groups of people by their race as evidenced chiefly by their skin color or other visible physical features are of superior intelligence and capabilities than others. To buttress their arguments white racists cite the fact that practically all the major achievements in the fields of engineering, theoretical and applied science, medicine, farming, literature and other fields have been the work of Europeans or people of European origins. For, to the extent that Americans are in the vast majority of European origin, the case of the racists superficially appears attractive and supported by the facts as currently known or thus known for the past five centuries.

However there are many major flaws and weaknesses in the assumptions of the racists which undermine their theory and practice of racism. A few are highlighted here.

First, the comparisons of the achievements of white and non-white races are purely subjective and Eurocentric. The yardstick and criteria that are used are in origin, concepts and structure, all European. There is no taking into account the concepts and systems of evaluation of non-Europeans. In other words the assessor is using his own language, customs, traditions and moral and other values to judge the other side.

Secondly, the comparisons, conveniently for the white man, are made dating from after the fifteenth century. For as Professor Jared Diamond states in his celebrated book: *Guns, Germs and Steel*, till after the fifteenth century all nations and peoples were roughly at about the same levels of technological development. Their creative achievements, taking into account environmental conditions were the same or similar. All peoples used simple farming tools, rowed their boats, relying on wind power, and inter alia, used simple and basic cooking utensils and sources of energy, such as fossil fuels.

Thirdly, the information about the achievements in science and mathematics by non-Europeans in the Middle Ages and before were deliberately or unwittingly suppressed or marginalized. This approach was necessary and needed to justify the so called inferiority of non-white people, thus providing the ideal rationalization for racism. After all, it makes sense for me to hide the noble works of say, 'green skinned people' and expose their negative works if I'm setting about to show that these 'green people' are inferior to black people and therefore cannot and must not be treated as equals of black people.

As a matter of fact this ingrained predisposition to discount the valuable contributions of nonwhite people to civilization is still evident in the developed world. For instance few white people know that Mathematics was first developed by nonwhites in India and that Timbuktu situated in the Sahara Desert was, in the ninth and tenth centuries, a magnificent center of learning to which great scholars and writers went to study. It was indeed the capital of the powerful and flourishing Ghana Empire till it was overrun by the Almoravids in 1075.

To many people of European extraction Timbuktu even now is associated with extreme remoteness and ignorance. Yet only a few centuries ago it was the equivalent of Harvard or Cambridge or Oxford of the twenty first century.

The harsh climatic conditions in Africa and Asia, particularly the former, have made it nigh impossible for learned documents, books and other materials to be stored and preserved as have been the case in the cold parts of the world. Hence the ridiculous idea has gained credence that Africans and Asians have contributed little or nothing to the progress of humanity and therefore are inferior to those where there is preserved evidence of their achievements.

As Dr. Jared Diamond clearly explains in his classic work on human development and progress it is the environment, and not race, as the racists love to perpetuate, that has led to the differences in advancement and progress between Europeans and non-Europeans.

And there is compelling evidence for this view from the fields of genetics, anthropology and history. The original human beings started on the plains of East Africa and then grew in numbers before they began to migrate for food, water or shelter or merely for exercise, as animals, especially mammals, still do up to this day.

The original human beings coming from the same parents must have had the same genetic constitutions. Therefore, any differences in capabilities or achievements over thousands of years must be attributable to the different conditions and challenges which the various migrant groups faced and had to overcome in order to survive.

Over thousands of years, the environmental conditions must have produced new adaptive characteristics and features to suit survival and life in the different geographic areas and the diverse climates. Thus the groups that moved northwards through North Africa and ended in Europe, with its cold climate had to develop noses with small constricted passages so that the cold air being breathed in was warmed before reaching the lungs. Equally, the people who migrated to hot areas needed broad noses to cool the air breathed in before it reaches the mouth.

Also as all human beings initially must have had the same skin pigmentation levels of the protective biochemical called melanin, it means that the groups who went to Europe where there is less sunshine per year than in Africa, over the millennia, with no sunshine to interact with the melanin, would be less and less dark than their siblings in Africa and Asia.

Furthermore, as the hair is an extension or part of the skin, and melanin exists in the skin, with the prolonged absence of sunshine the hair would ultimately over many millennia come to lose its dark coloration.

This view is not a mere hypothesis but is supported by visible facts. For instance, Europeans who are born and live in countries close to the Equator tend to be more dark-skinned than Europeans who live in northern Europe. Does this mean that those who live in northern Europe are more intelligent or more capable than their southern brothers and sisters? Certainly not! In fact, modern Western civilization, according to historians, archeologists and anthropologists began in southern Europe in the region of the Mediterranean Sea, and was influenced by its many connections with the peoples on the other side, the non-European Egyptians and Babylonians. This historic achievement underlines once more the vital role of the environment in determining the future and progress of various peoples or races.

Naturally, as the early human beings migrated into colder climates they must have been forced by the harsh cold to devise ways and means of clothing themselves to keep warm in order not to freeze to death. So even putting aesthetic considerations aside, they were forced to cover their nakedness with some form of covering however basic and primitive initially.

The same could be said for housing. The cold severe weather necessitated the need initially to live in caves and then over the thousands of years build structures that would protect them from the elements. So the criteria which for centuries have been used subjectively by Europeans to classify others as inferior are flawed ab initio. The racial differences are not and cannot be genetic as racists prefer to propagate but chiefly the responses over long periods of time by peoples to different environmental conditions.

Consequently, the need for the siblings living in hot sunny zones to develop big noses that could cool the hot air being breathed, dark skins to withstand the sun's strong ultraviolet rays, and to develop little clothing to allow for maximum ventilation of the whole body are easily explained by the environment.

The racists being white themselves have deliberately placed a subjective evaluation and interpretation on racial differences by classifying white as nice and good, black as ugly and bad. But there is no compelling, scientific evidence for such evaluation. It is all subjective and unfortunately for at least four centuries they were in the military position, emanating from technological advancement, to enforce their set of values on all peoples who were not European or of European extraction or did not physically look like them. So in effect the ideology of racism was being propagated through the barrel of the gun. Therefore those who did not have guns or better yet really powerful weapons capable of mass destruction, had little choice but to succumb and accept that they were inferior to the conqueror or victor.

However, it is in the field of intelligence evaluation that the theory and practice of racism are shown to be grossly flawed. And interestingly it has been on the so-called intelligence assessment or evaluation that racists have for centuries based their ideology. But their beliefs grounded on the comparisons of the achievements of European and non-European races do not pass the test of reason for the following reasons:

Those doing the assessment or evaluation use their own language, social customs, traditions and patterns of behavior as the yardstick. Achievements of non-Europeans are marginalized, suppressed or not taken into account.

The approach of the assessors is oddly akin to a criminal case in which the judge combines the roles of judge, prosecutor, devil's advocate, jury and court psychologist, with the son or brother of the judge being the accused. With a modicum of intelligence the outcome of the trial can be predicted even before it has begun. Yet for about five centuries (the fifteenth to mid twentieth century) this is what has been going on globally in the field of inter-racial relations.

By comparing the lives and achievements of whites and nonwhites, especially in the modern age, without any reference to the past histories and circumstances of the two major groups, the racists have been able to superficially appear to win the argument through highlighting the evident and palpable achievements of Europeans. They have failed wittingly or otherwise to recognize the roles of slavery, colonialism and genocide in the apparent underdevelopment of all non-white countries, apart from Japan.

More importantly, the white assessors or those in command and control positions have marginalized or completely ignored the huge impact of environmental conditions on the development and achievements of human beings.

However, in spite of the Eurocentric stance in evaluating the progress of the different races, despite the gross unfairness in the assessments and comparisons, the phenomenal achievements of non-Europeans, against the huge and nigh insurmountable odds and challenges that confront them, have been overlooked.

I have tried below to set out how two groups, black and white, subject to entirely different environmental conditions, come out in competitive, unbiased, objective examinations. Although the facts set out here are derived from experiences in Ghana, at a time when it was a British colony, there is no reason to doubt that they apply to other African or Asian countries. All of them at a period of their history were under European colonial rule.

## PRENATAL CARE AND ATTENTION

Since the twentieth century in the richer Western nations, white mothers get the benefit of proper care and attention from doctors and experienced consultants with regular medical checkups, including the supply of essential vitamins, minerals and milk. Appropriate exercises meant to strengthen the abdominal muscles and improve the general health of the mother-to be are included in the program.

As the health delivery is free and is carried even to those who for one reason or another are house-bound, there is no likelihood of any women in need being left without appropriate care and attention.

On the other hand, black mothers receive very little prenatal attention by doctors. if they are fortunate. At best they may get the services of a trained nurse or midwife or nurse-in training. The situation is better for those who live in the big towns or cities than for those in the rural areas, although the majority of the population in Ghana and other African countries live in the rural areas. In many countries of Asia, the conditions are similar to those in Ghana. Thus whilst there are twenty-seven doctors to ten thousand people in the UK, in India the figure is six and in Ghana one.[*]

## ANTE/POST-NATAL CARE

The mothers from the United Kingdom get the best of attention for free. Delivery of the baby is either at a hospital under optimal conditions, supervised by a doctor or midwife. There is even post-natal maternity leave or vacation thrown in at the expense of the state if needed. Regular visits to the mother and baby are carried out by a trained nurse, doctor or social worker.

As the mother and baby get stronger they go for regular checkups at the local hospital or clinic, free of charge. And if for one reason or another they cannot go to the hospital or clinic nearest to them, they are visited at home to ensure that their medical needs are addressed appropriately. Furthermore, in many cases, if after a professional evaluation by the visiting health worker he / she determines that the home conditions are not ideal for the baby and mother, then immediate action is taken to improve the situation.

For most mothers in Ghana and other countries in Africa and Asia, these ideal conditions do not exist. Even for those who live in towns and cities, health care before and after delivery is limited. Naturally those who cannot bear the long waiting time at the state or government hospitals or clinics and can afford to go private, do so. But they are a small minority.

Thus maternal mortality is unnecessarily high in Ghana and other developing countries for a natural process that should not cause any deaths at all. As deputy health minister of Ghana I was appalled by the figures that I read of preventable deaths. Sadly this depressing situation is repeated in many developing countries in Africa and Asia.

## NURSERY YEARS

In Britain and other developed countries, all white except Japan, the babies continue to get state funded health and medical attention,

---

[*] Source: Pocket World in Figures 2013 the Economist, London

including visits at home if necessary. Where the mother is working, the babies are placed in properly supervised nurseries, paid for in part or fully by the state.

Whether the mother is working or not, and the babies are at nurseries or at home, in all cases toys, pictures, books and other artefacts designed to improve body and mind are available for the babies to interact with. In the few cases where the mothers cannot afford the toys or the items essential for the proper upbringing and development of the babies or the father is delinquent, the state steps in to provide the needed clothes and toys for the babies. For many of the families in Africa and Asia such conditions and environments for optimal development of babies do not exist, excepting a few cases.

## ELEMENTARY AND PRIMARY SCHOOL YEARS

The children in the United Kingdom and other European countries are brought up in homes where they get wholesome and nourishing meals. Even for poor families, through the intervention of the state, the children get at least the basics needed for their proper growth and development.

In many cases the children are driven to school by their parents or accompanied there by one of their parents. School meals are provided for those in need, and school buses are available to convey the children to and from school.

School buildings amply supplied with textbooks, pens, pencils and other educational materials are situated within easy reach of the parents. Qualified teachers are on hand to cater for the welfare of the children. They also get regular visits from school doctors and psychologists.

Additionally there are ample facilities for physical and mental development such as sports fields, and libraries. Practically all of these are supervised by trained men and women. Outside activities such as outings to major places of historic, geographic or national interest are organized by many school authorities, to ensure that the children are exposed to major features of the environment as they grow up. These extracurricular activities go to supplement the learning at school. Their contribution to the advancement and progress of the children, both physical and psychological, must be enormous.

Sadly for many school children in Ghana and other African countries, and for others in Asia, the ideal conditions outlined above do not exist. No school transport, no school meals and no doctors. In many instances, the school buildings are shabby and are not adequately provided with text books and teachers. And in some remote rural areas classes are still held in the open air under trees. Under the fierce relentless sun it is amazing that the school children do not doze off, but are able to keep a lively interest in the classes.

To compound the huge problems that the children face during the rainy season, life becomes so unbearable that sometimes schools have to close for a few days. Meanwhile their white counterparts in Europe and the Americas continue with their education uninterrupted except by the intervention of delinquent irresponsible parents. But then the state, as represented by the education and law enforcement authorities, steps in to rescue the children and bring to prosecution the erring parents, usually fathers who have gone AWOL!

In a nutshell, white children are generally looked after and provided for in a way and manner that millions of children in Africa and Asia can only dream of. Every effort is made either by the parents or through state intervention to ensure that the potential of the child, both physical and mental, is developed to the maximum.

However, it is at the education and facilities provided for white children at secondary or high school level that the already huge gap in opportunities between the two groups becomes even wider and greater, reaching almost insurmountable conditions.

Apart from the congenial home environment that the white children enjoy, all the tools and facilities needed for progress and advancement are at their disposal. For example, their school buildings are well equipped, and are subject to regular inspections and repairs. Qualified teachers, books and other educational items are amply supplied.

The modest analysis below illustrates the enormous advantages which white students have over their black counterparts. Black students in Ghana, even when under the administration of the United Kingdom, and the experiences of other black students in other parts of Africa, were no different.

## STUDY OF SCIENCE

In most secondary schools in Africa, science and other laboratory equipment is very limited. For as the items have to be imported from overseas, their cost is considerable and often beyond the resources of many schools. Furthermore it should be noted that whilst their white counterparts have been familiar with science instruments from nursery school age, albeit as plastic toys, for most black students their first sight or interaction with basic equipment such as a Bunsen burner or a conical flask or microscope is when they enter a science laboratory for the first time at the age of eleven or twelve. *I must confess that I never saw a microscope till age twelve when I was fortunate to attend a well funded government boarding school. Indeed I was scared when I was asked to look into the insrument. Additionally, I was terrifiedof the science teacher whose skin looked very pink and I could see the blood in the veins of his hands.*

## MATHEMATICS

Although as with the science subjects, both groups may use the same textbooks printed and published in Great Britain, the white students generally have the advantage of better qualified staff. Also they have physical mathematical modules at their disposal which often the best secondary schools in Ghana and other African countries do not have to help them understand and visualize the relevant concepts.

## HISTORY/ SOCIAL STUDIES

In addition to the whole syllabus, being British based and oriented, the textbooks are more easily available to the white students than to the black students. Some of the teachers are the same people who wrote the textbooks. Thus the students get the chance to discuss aspects of the subject under study from the horse's own mouth, metaphorically speaking.

Before the end of the secondary school course, students are taken on visits to places of great historic interest such as the Houses of Parliament (Congress), where laws have been made for centuries, and go on outings to museums and galleries which further enrich and complement the knowledge acquired from textbooks and lectures.

Some of the more financially endowed schools or colleges even have visits from eminent writers, historians or public figures to encourage, enliven and motivate them. If even such visits do nothing at all for the students, surely the very interaction with outstanding and great personalities, however brief the duration, must have positive impacts on the students.

Students in African, Caribbean or Asian countries do not have the marvelous opportunities of immense value in the acquisition of knowledge and vital for personal development, mental and physical, enumerated above.

## GEOGRAPHY

Again the enormous advantages that the white students have over their black counterparts show themselves. The textbooks used by both groups preponderantly deal with topics that are very familiar to the white students but completely alien to the other group. For example, whilst the white students from birth become familiar with snow, the black students' only acquaintance with snow is what they read in the same geography books that both sides are using. They lack the benefit of physical contact and knowledge with the real thing. So they have no choice but to make do with paper snow.

On a serio-comic note may I state that like many African students of my generation (and we were among the privileged few) I never saw snow till the age of twenty four when I came to the United Kingdom as a student.

## ENGLISH /LITERATURE

From very early infancy white children are introduced to the English language by their mothers, through songs and the written word. Progressively, as they grow, they are encouraged and helped to develop their mastery of their mother tongue. I am here excluding the very tiny minority of parents who are delinquent in their parental duties.

Any deficiency in the education of the deprived children is suitably seen to by the intervention of the state, through the local social and education services. Practically all the secondary schools have well stocked libraries, adequate textbooks and good teachers. In the four year high school education they are taken on visits to the homes of Shakespeare and other historic writers. Eminent professors or other academics from nearby universities may drop in to give a lecture on aspects of the language or literature.

The black students, if they are fortunate, may be using the same textbooks but generally do not have the extra benefits alluded to above. Even where the teachers are as qualified as those in Britain or other European countries, they do not have the extra facilities like full comprehensive libraries and other facilities which go to enhance the education of the students.

It also needs to be taken into account the counselling and other services which are simply not available to the black students in Ghana, other African or Asian countries.

At the end of the four year course of studies the black and white students take the same examinations. Ghana, being on the same time zone as the United Kingdom, meant that both the students in Britain and in Ghana took the examinations on the same days and at the same time. The only difference was that a distance of three thousand, five hundred miles separated both groups.

It may interest readers to note the following:

*The examination questions were set, printed, packaged and dispatched to Ghana and other African countries by white British men.

*At their destinations the parcels were kept in secure safes by white men.

*All the invigilators at the examinations were white. The only black presence being the intimidating black academic gowns that they wore for the occasions.

*All the written answers by the students were collected, collated and conveyed (by sea or air) to Britain by white men.

*The sheets of answers, with no names on them but only the serial numbers of the students, were marked by white men and possibly women.

*Finally, independent of the markers, the relevant marks scored by each serial number were matched by the administration section of the examining board against the registered names of the students.

The whole examinations exercise was designed to ensure that as much as humanly possible there was no bias, prejudice, corruption dishonesty or undue influence. Certainly there was simply no way that the black students or their parents or school authorities could in any way influence the results of the examinations.

As such the results could not be faulted in any way. Even where there was an appeal system by any aggrieved school authorities to challenge some of the results as unfair or biased, the appeal process was cumbersome, expensive and time consuming. The appeals board members were all white and to my knowledge no African school or college ever lodged an appeal.

So by no stretch of the imagination could any person, black or white, argue convincingly that the examinations were skewed in favor of the black students. Therefore, the announced results must be true and accurate.

Consistently they showed that in many cases, the black students, with all the nigh insurmountable challenges and difficulties they had to grapple with, scored as good a marks as the white students and often achieved even higher scores. What is even more amazing and must give much food for thought to white academics and writers, who cannot unburden themselves of racism, is the fact that in English Language and Literature and in British History, some black students obtained higher marks than their white counterparts, despite the huge advantages that the latter were bestowed with from birth, at home, at school and even on the playing fields. In fact, if all the white students achieved A's (that is seventy percent and above) it should come as no surprise at all to any rational fair-minded person, given their advantages. However, this was not the case!

If a student who has been speaking English and dreaming in English, emotionally and psychologically acquainted with the language and given all the necessary academic tools and stimuli for his advancement takes the same test or examination with his black counterpart who started English at age five and all his life has to think, speak and work in English with his mother tongue competing all the time in his mind for recognition, what results could rationally be predicted?

Indeed, considering the overwhelming odds and challenges that black students face in Africa or Asia, it is incredible why most of them do not fail the examinations or do badly in a competitive life, assessed almost entirely by white Anglo-Saxon males (WASPS)

Even the least cursory review of these results, extrapolated a thousand times all over Africa, Asia, the Caribbean Islands and Asia-Pacific must convince the most rabid racist that the fundamental basis of racism, namely that nonwhite people, are inferior or less intelligent or capable, is flawed. As a matter of fact, Dr. Jared Diamond goes further to state that after over thirty years of detailed studies of nonwhite people in the Pacific Region, he has come to the conclusion that nonwhite people are more clever than white people. Interestingly, Dr. Jared is an eminent, white American geography/sociologist/writer. It must take a considerable amount of intellectual courage to make such a statement, which goes against the grain of conventional wisdom among many white intellectuals in Europe and America. Naturally it's very difficult for most people, black or white, to place truth and professional honesty above ephemeral personal interests. So for several decades the hallowed 'facts' white racists (including some renowned academics and intellectuals) have been peddling have actually been self-serving myths, namely the inferiority of the black people.

With the relevant physical and military power to back their pseudoscience and unchallenged ideas and ideologies, they have done immense and cataclysmic damage not only to their own people but to hundreds of millions of people the world over.

Whilst it would be wrong and fallacious to conclude from the academic results referred to above that nonwhite people are more intelligent or smarter than white people, the least that can be rationally be deduced from these results is that nonwhite people put under the same or identical examinations, with no element of bias or subjectivity, can perform as well as white people. That is assuming that those who are doing the examinations or evaluations, whether in the fields of science, medicine, engineering or the liberal arts are not influenced by factors that favor one group or another.

However the racists appear to have a case when they point to the fact that certainly since the nineteenth century, beginning with the industrial revolution, practically all the major achievements in science, medicine, engineering and the arts have been by white people. But the weakness of this argument may be summarized as follows: First, these outstanding records and the non-performance of the nonwhite races do not take into account the centuries of slavery and colonialism suffered by nonwhite people from the hands of white people.

Secondly, the achievements referred to above were recorded by Europeans or white people (including Americans) but particularly by those living in Northern Europe and North America. Does this mean that the white people or Europeans in the south of Europe or outside the United States are less clever or intelligent than those in the northern, colder regions of the Europe? Certainly not, although at the apogee of the Nazi theories on race there were many powerful academics, intellectuals and opinion formers who thought so. Sadly the cataclysmic consequences of the implementation of such unscientific and baseless ideologies were not limited to the perpetrators only but also to millions of people in all parts of the world, including the victims of racism. Tragically, by the time such a dangerous ideology was expunged from the earth and consigned to the dustbins of history, incalculable damage and harm had been done.

Even seven decades after the horrendous and apocalyptic experience, humanity continues to suffer the side effects and repercussions, in various forms and shapes.

Readers may be interested in an important documentary program that was aired by the BBC (British Broadcasting Corporation) in 2013. Well researched, it was a three part documentary which tried to answer the question why the Industrial Revolution began in the nineteenth century in no other European country other than the United Kingdom. The firm conclusion was that the historic epoch making achievement of Britain at that material time was the result of a combination of factors, not as a result of the innate superior intelligence of white British people. These factors were: 1. Availability of coal, 2. Proximity to water, 3. Access to iron from the colonies, and 4. the liberal intellectual climate of the period, which encouraged free untrammeled thinking, without the intervention of the state to stifle the creative imagination and expression of views and ideas. In other words there existed in Britain in the nineteenth century far more freedom of thought than elsewhere in Europe. This situation encouraged many minds to blossom and flourish. Hence, can be explained the great scientific, medical and engineering achievements of the period. This enlightened attitude was hard won in the seventeenth century struggles of the English Parliament against the tyranny of the King. Thinkers like John Locke paved the way for toleration and the rights of the individual to free speech. And once a country, group of nations or race have a head start, although catching up by the rest is not impossible, it is not at all easy, especially when those who are ahead naturally do not want to lose their advantage or relinquish what they have come to enjoy.

# CHAPTER 5

# THE THREE GREAT MYTHS

For several decades, white racists, whilst maintaining that nonwhites are less capable, less intelligent and less successful than Caucasians have abided by three major stereotypes. These have become so ingrained as to command the status of firm facts. The myths are as follows: 1. Black people are only good at sports. 2. Black people are only good at music and 3. Black people, especially the men, are sex-driven. Any genuine and serious effort to contribute towards the eradication of racism must therefore examine these 'hallowed fairytales' which for long have masqueraded as facts. Even educated white people, with no racist intentions or motives tend to take them for granted as self-evident. So it should be useful to examine the so-called facts and see whether they stand the test of reason.

Sports

I am here including all the major, competitive physical activities in these fields: football, athletics, tennis, basketball, swimming and boxing. It is true that from the results at all the major sports competitions, black people tend to do better than whites or Caucasians. But this, I humbly submit, is not due to an inherent genetic disposition or characteristic but to purely environmental conditions. The following observations are germane to the argument:

1. Black people do not do exceptionally well in all the sports but mostly in those which do not require long periods of expensive

training. Thus apart from the Williams sisters from the United States of America and Arthur Ashe, also of America, there have been few such outstanding success stories from black tennis players. Again, notwithstanding the historic record of Tiger Woods, it would be safe and correct to state that there have not been many outstanding black golf heroes. For these and other sports activities are not only difficult to get into, but require a large investment of money and time in order to shine in and achieve fame.

On the other hand, activities such as running, jumping, boxing and football do not require the same levels of cash investment in training and career progression as the expensive sports. Thus whilst it is fairly easy in Africa for a young lad to start a profession in football playing initially barefooted and with no jersey and no proper playing field, the same cannot be said for golf or tennis. Many black football players from Africa who later became famous and wealthy in Europe began their lives on playing fields that by European standards would have been closed down and no sports doctors or psychologists were ever present to boost the player's efforts.

All black runners who achieve international fame and wealth started doing cross country running, or marathons bare footed, with little or no training. Certainly they did not have the benefit of professional coaches, doctors and nourishing, vitamin-fortified meals to live on. All they had to rely on initially were their bare feet and stamina. As such when, after such grueling experiences, black athletes come to compete in Europe, either as residents or visitors, with all the almost idyllic conditions, they naturally feel that they are almost in Paradise and thus have no excuse whatsoever not to be first or among the first. Furthermore, all the black athletes, whether consciously aware or not, know at the back of their minds that the spectators, predominantly white, would be judging the whole black race by what they achieve on the fields. This expectation makes them try all the harder.

The same can be said about an activity in which black people have done exceptionally well—boxing. Again this is a field which does not need a long and expensive course of training and other requirements such as special clothes, at least not in the initial stages.

It may be noted here that generally black people are poorer than white people, so it has not been possible for them to shine in sports such as tennis or golf. For even the parents with children that showed a talent or aptitude in these sports, the challenges posed by insufficient finance have not been easy to overcome.

This, in my considered view, explains the absence of great tennis players in all of the United States of America, excluding the Williams sisters and a few others such as Arthur Ashe. I do not think that the fact that few black people have shone in tennis or golf (excluding Tiger Woods, of course) means that nonwhite people have a genetic disposition towards such lack of success.

There is no reason why white people, with the necessary determination training and stamina cannot be outstanding boxers or runners. That in a few cases white boxers have openly beaten black boxers and white runners have outshone black runners goes to suggest that both racial groups are capable of outstanding achievements and that race or skin color cannot be a factor in such achievements or failures.

So whilst it is true to state that black sportsmen do better than their white counterparts, the truer and more encompassing appraisal should be that black people do better in the sports that do not require too much investment in time, money and other resources. For in the fields of sports, as in other human endeavors, success is closely correlated to the availability of finance and other resources, even if both parties, black and white, have the same interest or talent or aptitude. If black racists claim or argue that black people have special inborn qualities that account for their undisputed records in certain sports then they should not be surprised if white racists turn round and argue that the epoch making achievements of Caucasians in science, medicine, engineering, cosmology, astrophysics and other fields amply suggest that white people have special genetic qualities that account for such success. The English have a saying: "You can't have your cake and eat it." I think that the wisdom behind this saying is very apt to the argument above.

## Music/Entertainment

In this field, black people also, in spite of all the huge, almost insurmountable difficulties and challenges that they have faced for centuries and continue to encounter, have done fantastically well. Michael Jackson, Jimi Hendrix, Stevie Wonder, Eartha Kitt, Shirley Bassey, Aretha Franklin and many others may be mentioned here. Again it would be noticed that these great achievements are in the genre of music or entertainment which do not require long and expensive training, preparation and supervision.

But in the types of music or entertainment which require very long and expensive training and preparation to reach national or international acclaim such as opera, classical music or ballet, the ratio of black singers or entertainers has not been so spectacular. Of course, there have been quite a few US opera stars like Margaret Tynes, Leontyne Price, the Maori-New Zealander Dame Kiri Te Kanawa and a few others. Still it is safe to state that their numbers do not compare at all with the achievements chalked up in popular music. The issues of money and other resources referred to above equally apply here.

It may also be noticed that despite the challenges posed by racism, nonwhite singers or entertainers do exceptionally well in the types of music which have a popular appeal, where the attraction or success of the music depends far more on the evaluation of the mass audience than on the assessment of music critics or experts, who invariably are white. Thus a popular song performance to an overwhelmingly white audience by a black singer or performer will earn huge approval and commendation irrespective of what the music critics might say or write. The audience have immense input in the assessment of how they like the music and what music they will buy. On the other hand the fate of a performance of classical music or opera or ballet can be greatly influenced by the verdicts of the critics, which are purely subjective. It is therefore safe to state that in the spheres of entertainment or sports where the evaluation of the results or outcome are subject to minimal or no subjective element on the side of the 'expert' assessors or evaluators, nonwhites do well and are seen to do very well.

For instance, if in a boxing match all the judges are white and the referee is white and assuming out of racial prejudice they have been scoring unfavorably against the black boxer, if there is a knock out, with all the white spectators watching there is no way that the judges can rule in favor of the white boxer, if even they try.

Similarly, in let's say an open event of running, with all the white spectators seeing with their own eyes that the black runner is leading with the white runners trailing behind, it would be difficult for any rational judge of the event to announce that the white runner won!

It means that because of racism, for the avoidance of any doubts, whenever there are competitions involving black and white people, the black candidates have to exhibit incontrovertible evidence of success over their white counterparts. Furthermore, evaluation of the results should be open and transparent, and involve the minimum subjective assessment from the judges or assessors. Under such ideal conditions no loser, black or white, can blame anyone but himself.

For any assessments of the various achievements or failures to be meaningful, the playing field must be smooth and fair to both sides. Otherwise, to use the results of comparisons based on one advantaged group over the other becomes an exercise in futility. In China, Japan and South Korea, the governments have been eager for their nationals to shine and have supported their training. As a result, their classical musicians are today among the most outstanding in the world.

## SEX

Another myth that has for centuries been used to demonize black men and has served as one of the major props of racism is the view that black men are sexually very potent and that part of the reason for the underdevelopment of black countries is that the men are obsessed with sex, thus leaving less time and energy for other pursuits like education and personal advancement.

The supposed evidential support for this view is the fact that black people have indeed more children than white people. Whether in a biracial population like the United States of America or in an almost homogenous society such as the United Kingdom, the facts and figures show black people have more children than their white compatriots. For example, in both the USA and the U.K the rate of children born outside marriage is about five times higher than in the white community. But it serves no useful purpose to merely state the facts and figures and deduce from them that nonwhite men are more sexually disposed. An honest and rational approach to an appraisal of the figures must examine and delve deeply into causes of the figures. And it would be found, if impartially undertaken, that there is no racial or genetic dimension to the problem. The truth behind the higher birth figures and higher rates of out of marriage births lie in the following explanations. They have no race bias or proclivity.

1. As white populations have higher levels of education and disposable incomes than black countries they do have indeed fewer children than black people. But even in a homogenous white or black population those with higher incomes and higher education do have less children than their less fortunate compatriots. Therefore, the multiplicity of children has nothing to do with race.

2. All the poor or developing countries are in Asia, Africa, The Pacific Region, the Caribbean Islands and South America. In all these countries religion and time hallowed traditions do not encourage the use of contraception. This situation therefore leads to large families.

3. Even if people in these areas of the world were disposed to the use of contraception, as many people are poor, earning less than two dollars a day to live on, contraceptives become very

difficult to afford. Their purchase is thus trumped by such vital essentials like food, water, clothing and shelter.

4. Child mortality has always been high in poorer nations and so people had more children knowing that many would probably die. Children were also an investment in terms of labor and security for old age, in the absence of government social security and welfare programs.

5. In all these countries generally, having a large family is a sign of wealth and prestige, as was the case in Europe right up to the early part of the twentieth century. It is education and rapidly changing economic conditions that have led to the drastic reduction in the sizes of families in countries where the overwhelming majority of the population are white or European. As the levels of education and incomes grow in the black or developing countries, the same phenomenon, namely reduction in family sizes, becomes evident.

Finally, on the so-called sexual prowess of black men, it may interest readers to learn that as a deputy minister of health in Ghana I had the opportunity to read about cases of male sexual dysfunction and other problems. What I came across and from subsequent study have convinced me that black males are no more sexually aggressive or predisposed than others. The myth of their sexual potency has been perpetrated by white racists, as part of the program and campaign to demonize them and justify racism.

Of course, this myth also arose as a reaction of Christians in particular. Sexual shame and self-discipline had long been part of Christianity and was particularly prominent in nineteenth century England (under the prudery encouraged by Queen Victoria), at the very time that English colonists were moving to Africa. There they were shocked to observe an entirely different culture which was less sexually repressive than their own. Instead of understanding that the difference in behaviors was culturally inscribed, they drew the false conclusion that the black man was a sexual maniac. I suppose at that time they did not have the benefit of Freudian analysis to understand their own unconscious motives and projections of their shadow side onto the hapless black man!

For if they could convincingly make the case that black males are sexual predators or people with insatiable sexual appetites then there is a strong justification in ostracizing them or treating them with a good measure of hatred.

In conclusion, the significantly higher numbers of children per family, either from marriages or outside are correlated to levels of incomes, education, religion and traditions. There is no race element whatsoever. The anatomy and physiology of all peoples being the same, excluding skin color due to melanin levels, it is difficult to argue that nonwhite males are sexually more potent than others. To maintain otherwise does not stand the test of reason. In fact such a posture thus becomes racism in reverse. There is no evidence whatsoever that black men are exempt from masculine health problems such as erectile dysfunction, low sperm count, impotence and low libido.

CHAPTER 6

# ECONOMIC AND POLITICAL EFFECTS OF RACISM ON BLACK PEOPLE

Three major deleterious effects of racism may be discerned. They are economic, social and political. Wherever racism has been practiced it has led to the retardation in the economic development and progress of the victims. Thus in the colonies of Europeans in Africa, Asia or the Caribbean area, the local people were not encouraged to build factories even where the necessary raw materials were available. Although Ghana was for several decades the leading producer of cocoa beans, there was not a single factory in existence during the colonial period to process the cocoa beans. It was only in 1951 when an indigenous black government came into power that the anomaly was addressed. Ultimately, against the negative frightening advice of numerous white experts and advisors, the first chocolate factory was built in 1964 in Tema and later a second one in Takoradi. Since then, Ghana-made chocolates have won awards and prizes in international, blind, unbiased, objective competitions and assessments.

The improvements in the national economy, increased provision of jobs and the rise in the quality of life of the people have been considerable. Sadly, not all African states had the caliber of leadership to move their people forward in spite of the challenges in their path posed by racism. The argument is often made that as the colonial eras ended over sixty years ago by now the baneful effects of the system should have been overcome. In theory this should be the case but in practice, when a system has gone on for generations it is not at all easy to eradicate its legacy.

This is especially the case if the leaders want to introduce and practice a multiparty democratic system of governance. So whilst it is possible in a dictatorship for the leaders, by force or the threat of force, to mobilize large numbers of adults to work on the construction of factories, from dawn to dusk, (as took place under the Stalinist tyranny) such an option is not available to the political leaders committed to democracy. The colonial powers were only interested in removing raw materials, not in fostering indigenous manufacturing which would compete with their own, so the underdevelopment of the former colonies is crystal clear. In other words, the racism that existed in these countries has a correlation with the levels of economic development.

Without any shadow of doubt, democracy is far preferable to dictatorship, from the right or left of the political spectrum. From a long term perspective, by any yardstick or criteria, democracy is better than dictatorship. However, it is equally important that in a democracy, with a history of economic underdevelopment engineered by racism, a well-grounded mechanism is worked out and introduced which motivates the people to work hard and with dedication, both as volunteers or employees, without unduly compromising their human rights.

The economies of all the countries populated by nonwhite people still rely heavily on agriculture and the export of raw produce or unprocessed minerals such as gold, diamonds, copper, bauxite and oil. So long as this economic situation continues, the countries that produce them will remain poor or developing. This dire state of underdevelopment plays into the hands of racists. For however weird and illogical their stance, they can point to the fact that the economic and industrial development levels of the black nations is still way behind theirs. Of course, they ignore the fact that they are blaming the victim for the very situation which their former governments are chiefly responsible for.

The immense damage done to countries that suffer racism is palpable and concrete, but equally damaging has been the psychological effects of racism. They are invisible but nevertheless real. If anything at all they are more difficult to eradicate than the visible damage caused in the fields of the national economies or infrastructure. For with good economic planning and fiscal management, buttressed by national dedication to hard work, factories can be built in a matter of a few years, if the natural and mineral resources are available. But psychological damage is rather more challenging to remove or destroy and its effects are inter-generational.

The reasons for this difficulty are twofold. First, even though the negative impact of racism on the victim maybe invinsible, it is nevertheless real and deep seated.

Secondly, after decades or centuries of racism, many of the victims come to believe or accept their so-called inferior position in society. This is especially the case if the victims lack enlightened leadership and are not educated, thus easily prone to accept without challenge what they are told or shown by the racists. Of course, the damage can indeed be undone but must necessarily take some time, (at least a couple of generations), and would require considerable investments in the funding of mass education programs in addition to a restructuring of formal education at all levels, primary, secondary and tertiary.

For the debilitating effects and consequences of racism on the victims are so holistic and pervasive and so long lasting that only a robust and positive multi-pronged attack can produce the desired results. It is not going to be easy but it is not impossible if there is the political will!

The extent that many black women are prepared to go to lighten or whiten their skins is indicative of the psychological damage that racism has done to some of them. Not only are the creams and lotions that are used very corrosive and expensive but they end in many cases doing considerable damage to the upper epidermis of the skin ,producing in some hideous sores . In a few cases terrible ulcers have resulted  needing medical attention. As deputy health minster (secretary) of Ghana I sadly came across a few of such unnecessary damage to the skin by quite pretty women. And they had paid for damaging their skins All for what?

Considering that as the saying goes,' Beauty lies in the eyes of the beholder', it is rather sad that some black women as a result of sustained and relentless psychological pressure have come to feel that they are only beautiful if  they look white!

Whilst in all the cases cited above and others the unfortunate women are responsible for  their own predicament , we cannot ignore the responsibility of  all those who had created by diverse ways and means, the environment that made  the women feel that black is not beautiful.

However, the propagation of racism primarily affects its victims but also ironically harms and damages its perpetrators. There is an old saying that if a person throws dirt at someone a bit of the dirt sticks on the fingers of the thrower. Vindication of this aphorism is exemplified by the negative effects of racism on racists. Racism impacts negatively on racists in the following ways as outlined in the next chapter.

# CHAPTER 7

# ECONOMIC AND POLITICAL BURDEN OF RACISM ON WHITE PEOPLE

Where say a company or corporation infused with racism, as a policy, prefers to employ less qualified and less experienced white people than nonwhites with better qualifications and experience, in the long term such a policy, although appearing clever and smart, at the end of the day works to the detriment of the corporation. For the cumulative long term effects of using less competent people would cause negative financial consequences for the company.

Indeed, in the worst case scenario, some of the employees or at least one of them may make a serious professional or technical mistake that would land the company in a major lawsuit. The resulting huge loss in fines or time or detrimental impact on corporate image can be disastrous - all because racism and not professional competence was the yardstick for employment by the company or institution.

Another way in which racism can adversely affect the perpetrator is demonstrated by the great need of manufactured goods and expertise by the nonwhite countries, excluding Japan. All these nations, although developing industrially at varying speeds, would for some decades require expertise and machinery, which are predominantly in the developed countries, which are all white or Caucasian. So if a white country becomes notoriously identified as racist in its employment or administrative policies, it risks losing considerable volumes of exports to the black nations. Admittedly, the volume of exports from Europe and America to Africa, Asia and other nonwhite countries is not as great and significant as to the white countries. But even so, a boycott of goods from a country perceived as racist would negatively impact the economy of the country concerned. And as the peoples in the nonwhite countries become more educated, better organized as societies, and less prone to internal conflicts, their capacity to inflict economic damage on racist countries will naturally grow.

However small the economic damage, I maintain that it is grossly unfair and inhuman for any person or groups of persons in command and control positions to institute and implement policies that would lead to economic or financial suffering by some of their fellow citizens. Why should a decent hard worker in a factory, with himself and possibly a family to support, lose his job because the factory bosses are perceived and identified as racist and this has led to the factory going on reduced production, due to diminished exports to their African, Pacific, and Asian markets?

In fact, in a situation like this the employees who have lost their jobs would be completely justified to start 'a' class action in the courts against their bosses (directors and management) for their constructive dismissal. And I am sure that such legal proceedings against institutional racism would succeed and result in heavy damages and compensation costs. A few of such cases would make many employers, be they major, private or public institutions think several times before gleefully introducing and promoting racist policies and programs. In other words, forget about the victims of racism, it is simply not in the long term economic interest of predominantly white owned companies or corporations to advance racism. Superficially, racism may appear to be to their advantage but this is an illusion, with serious consequences that may not be short term but certainly long term.

Another economic factor working against racism, which appears to be frequently ignored by white racists, is the growing and rapid industrialization of many nonwhite countries. Thus the decades old monopoly of industrialized nations, all white except Japan, as the sole or main suppliers or providers of badly needed scientific and technical expertise and knowledge, and manufactured goods and machinery, is rapidly disappearing. For instance, apart from some very high-tech and super sophisticated machinery and equipment, vitally needed for national economic survival and security, there are no other goods and items that are not being manufactured by some nonwhite country. Thus, whilst for decades peoples in Africa relied solely on cars and vehicles imported from Europe and America, such items can now be obtained from South Korea, Malaysia, China, Brazil, India and Japan.

They now look to these countries for medicines, educational materials, heavy industrial machinery and advanced science equipment, such as super computers, cyclotrons or nuclear power stations. So white or European or Caucasian leaders in all spheres of life who wittingly or unwittingly promote racism or turn a blind eye to it in their midst, glibly saying that "they do not see color" when it is obvious and clear before them, are not fully aware of the harm and damage that they are doing to their countries and fellow citizens. At best they may be viewed as misguided patriots, or at worst as enemies of their people, seemingly espousing and promoting patriotism and the national interest. For in reality their racist activities do generate huge economic repercussions on their countries and peoples.

Of course, the diehard racists may argue that they do not need to trade or do business with the nonwhite nations. But this is not a true assessment of the global economic condition. For apart from the richest and most powerful nation in the world, namely the United States of America, where exports account for only about 14 percent of the national economy, no developed nation can continue to maintain its current high standard of living and quality of life without exports. And where currently their exports are to mostly other developed countries it means that over a period of time, perhaps a couple of decades, they would need to find other export markets. These are all in countries which are populated by nonwhite people. For the people in the developing countries account for about 85% of the global population.

Even going by the number of countries in the world, out of the two hundred nations, only 25% are white or of European extraction. The higher figure than the population figure is accounted for by the fact that Europe, although small in area, is divided into numerous independent countries. Thus two African nations, Algeria (area 2.4million sq.km) and the Democratic Republic of the Congo, D.R.C. (area, 2.35 sq.km) are together as large as the whole of Western Europe.

Another indication of the heavy reliance of the economies of the Western developed countries on the nonwhite nations is the fact that most of their heavy industries and other industrial activities are dependent on raw materials from the developing nations particularly those in Africa and the Middle East. For with its vast natural and mineral resources barely exploited, the continent of Africa, the cradle of humanity, is in a position to influence considerably the national economies of the white nations. Of course, the United States of America, with its vast and huge resources, natural and mineral, totally literate work force and its huge and heterogeneous population is not as dependent on the black nations for raw materials as others. But this position is unique in the whole world.

So as the global economy is structured now, whilst the developing countries, all nonwhite, can get their major essentials for their national economic development from nonwhite nations, the white nations are not in the position to do without the resources and raw materials from the black nations. That is, untill they develop alternative sources of fuel, raw materials and essential minerals such as gold, diamonds, molybdenum titanium, platinum, cobalt, bauxite, iron, uranium and others. Sixty percent of the strategic minerals of the world are in Africa alone.

It may interest readers to note that Africa alone accounts for 16.8 percent of the world's proven reserves of uranium, a vital element in the production of nuclear weapons and the mainstay of the nuclear power industry. With more comprehensive exploration it is possible that more deposits of this radioactive element, which underpins the whole nuclear industry for peaceful and military purposes will be found in the continent of Africa, which to date has shown that it contains almost unlimited minerals absolutely vital for modern civilization. Already the continent of Africa alone accounts for 16.8 % of the known uranium deposits worldwide. It is likely that future exploration will prove that the continent has more deposits of this vital element.

Also to be taken account of is the growing need of investors for facilities and opportunities for their funds. Admittedly, Europe and America continue to be the desired investment destinations. But with the passage of time the countries in Africa, Asia and the Pacific region will become more attractive for investors, as these nations offer more yields on investments. There are huge and very attractive investment opportunities in Africa that have hardly been touched. Indeed, Africa's potential is so great that what has already been exploited is just the tip of the iceberg.

Thus in the exploration of oil and gas, solar energy, wind power, nuclear power and the development of infrastructure and housing more investment opportunities exist in Africa than in Europe and the Americas. For example, whilst many house builders in Europe get, with luck, about 20 percent profit on their operations, in Ghana, the figure can be as high as 100 or 150 percent. That is, if the foreign investor and his company employees are prepared to put up with the hot and humid weather and the frequent visitations of the mosquitoes. But then in the modern age, with air conditioning and effective anti-malaria drugs and medicines the major environmental challenges should not be insurmountable, and indeed the Chinese government is already very active in this area.

So a white racist who is prevented from investing in Africa or any of the countries inhabited by nonwhite peoples because of his ideology and bigotry or feels that the nonracist political climate in those countries is not suitable for his bigotry or feels he might get into trouble for his racist views and therefore prefers to invest elsewhere for less returns ends up doing himself considerable economic and financial damage, especially so if his funds are heavily generated from loans or overdrafts.

Another serious economic damage that racists bring on their countries without being aware of, is their sabotage of the diplomatic efforts and work of their own diplomats abroad. All the developed nations, all white (bar Asian nations) spend hundreds of millions of dollars every year maintaining trade missions and embassies, with trade sections staffed by dedicated men and women who are prepared to go to 'hardship posts'. These men and women tirelessly work to promote trade and business for their countries.

By their successful work their countries secure more export or volumes of imports of badly needed raw materials for the factories back home. Their work under rather challenging conditions is greatly hampered if reports are circulated worldwide by radio, television and the print media that a prominent writer, journalist, or politician or academic has issued a statement that the peoples in those countries are stupid and unintelligent because they are black! The repercussions of such a report, irrespective of its consequences on the aggrieved people, would be to the considerable detriment of the country concerned. How big the damage would of course depend on the seriousness of the statement, the publicity that it receives, the status of the person that gave vent to his inner feelings with careless abandon and finally, the damage limitation that follows such a statement and by whom.

This small illustration shows the extent of the injury to the national interests that can be done by a single white racist or group to the overall economic interest of the country of which he is a member. In a situation as outlined above, wouldn't the diplomats or better still, the government of their compatriots, demand at the very least, as a matter of urgency, that the culprit gives them a cogent explanation or defense for the gross embarrassment and damage that he has caused his fellow countrymen? For by that single statement or book or pamphlet of his, he has alone, or with others, undermined the good work paid for by the taxpayers that is being done. Additionally, the freewheeling racist has diverted the attention of the diplomats from their work to defend the indefensible. Furthermore, the culprit has put at risk the jobs of possibly a few or more compatriots, without due cause or reason.

The consequences of the Second World War should serve us a vivid reminder to all human beings of the horrendous danger that racism poses and the enormous damage that it can cause the whole world, including ironically the perpetrators themselves.

From the perspective of many educated nonwhite peoples can be seen the writing on the wall, namely, that racism will ultimately rebound on its originators and perpetrators, if it is not eradicated as a matter of great national urgency. Therefore, any efforts by powerful people in command and control positions either to cover up cases of racism, or turn a blind eye, or trivialize them are in effect building a huge burden of racial and social challenges for their children and grandchildren. It is my humble submission that people should not create situations that would make life difficult and challenging for those whom they are responsible for now or in the future.

# CHAPTER 8

# GLOBAL EFFECTS OF RACISM

In every country where racism exists there are laws against it. For it is realised that racism is not only wrong and immoral but also against human decency. What is often not appreciated is the cumulative and deleterious repercussions of racism. Even where the politicians and opinion leaders are unhappy about the harm done to nonwhite minorities in their midst, they appear not to be mindful of the economic consequences of racism outside their territorial borders. As emphasized already, outside Europe and the Americas, the rest of the world is populated overwhelmngly by peoples who are not white or of European extraction.

This being the reality, geopolitically it is rather counterproductive for the minority group, race-wise, to institute and gaily promote a programme or ideology that in the long term is manifestly not in their best interest. True, in the short term racism offers enormous advantages to white people. The question is whether it is prudent and pragmatic to sacrifice major, long term vital interests for relatively brief, ephemeral interests, especially if the latter are subject to external factors outside the control of racists. For the effects of racism on the perpetrators are not only economic but psychological, with devastating results for the racist, outside the harm done to the victims of racism.

I submit that no person is born a racist. Racism is not an inherited characteristic like myopia or haemophilia. The behaviour is traceable predominantly 1, to parents through their example to their children 2, the school or 3, the work place. Of these three, the first, in my humble opinion, is the most important. Thus if a child is from birth exposed to racist language or patterns of bevaviour by the parents, he is bound as he grows to imbibe the example he was forced to observe in the home. And if this influence on his life grows unchecked and develops then, who should be blamed if as a young man, he behaves or says something in public that is considered racist and puts him on the wrong side of the law? Who is to blame? For parents are responsible for their children and not vice versa, surely.

That children imitate what they see, hear and feel may be illustrated by this small but true experience of mine. A few years ago, the nanny of a white university couple, both scientists with the husband a university professor at Chicago, visited us one morning. The little boy of fifteen months shook my hand and turned it over and was puzzled obviously why the palm of my hand looked like his but the back of my hand was different. This was legitimate innocent curiosity on the part of my little friend of less than two years. Naturally, if the white nanny and the parents at that age told him or made him understand that the black colour was because I am stupid and unintelligent and so are all such people and that only those whose hands are white are intelligent and clever, than naturally he would grow into a strong healthy white male, infused with the racism of his parents.

On the other hand if the parents patiently explain to him that the black colour is due to the fact that such people were born or come from countries where there is a lot of sunshine, or originally came from such countries, and the color acts as a prortection to their skin from being harmed by the strong sun, and that they are not superior or inferior to white people for that reason, then the little boy would grow into a healthy white American, devoid of racism and bigotry. He would be fully prepared by his parents to fit into a world in which overwhelmingly most of the peoples are not of his skin colour.

It is a pleasure to report here that my little friend, with the right example from his parents, grew into a bright young white man, who subsequently joined the foreign service of his country. Sadly, not all white children have received the benefit of such parental care, guidance and attention. Hence the reported cases in the media of some white men getting into trouble in their work place or playing fields, as a result of the indoctrination, formal or informal, which they received in childhood. The youth who gets into trouble for racist remarks or behaviour must not be blamed. It is the parents who ought to carry the blame.

Admittedly there are cases all over the world where parents of whatever colour or socioeconomic group have done their best for their children, with maximum love, affection and parental guidance and yet the children have fallen astray. They drifted either into drugs, drinking, smoking, promiscuity or other anti social behaviour. Despite these known cases it is still safe to say that children learn, good or bad, from their parents. The fact that a few small numbers of children, despite good parental care, love and example unfortunately end badly does not and should not mean that parental guidance and example do not bring expected results. After all, the English have an adage, 'One swallow does not make a summer', 'There are a few bad apples in every barrel'.

Even more dangerous to the children, devoid of moral parental care and guidance, is the risk they run as adults of missing out on a very good job or promotion for which they are eminently qualified, all because they talked or behaved or acted in a way and manner that was considered or deemed racist or smacking of racism at an interview. For as the global economy becomes more integrated and the world becomes a smaller and smaller village, with major events in countries impacting on each other, even racist employers, be they major corporations or government institutions, are gradually coming to the realisation that a white employee who is overtly racist is a big liability. For looming at the back of the minds of the comapany directors or managers is the understanding that an employee who demonstrates his racism by word or deed will attract on the company unwanted and negative publicity. He may cause the corporation an expensive law suit, possibly ending in heavy damages and compenasation payments.

Even an out of court settlement of legal proceedings against the company or institution may cost them some good money. Thus, whichever way the company looks at the problem on racism it simply is not in its overall interest to accommodate it or in one way or another be seen to accept it. Even in the best scenario if the corporation or institution wins a case of racism lodged against it, the time, energy and resources deployed in their totality to effect such an outcome would clearly establish that it would have been far cheaper and less stressful to have implemented institutional programmes and activities designed to avoid the original cause of the court case.

I use "overtly" advisedly, for in a democracy there is no law or can be no law that controls or regulates the inner feelings of free human beings. First, such a law would be phsically impossible to administer. Second, it would constitute an infringement on the human rights of the person. As such even in the countries with the strictest anti-racism laws and accompanying law enforcement procedures all that the law requires of the citizen or resident or any person subject to the jurisdiction of the state in question is that he must not translate his covert racism, if any, into overt racism. For that would attract consequences in the form of sanctions. They may take the form of a reprimand and caution, or a fine, sentence of community service or imprisonment.

This being the situation in even the most democratic of countries, the question is whether it is right for parents to inculcate into their children or wards ideas and views which in the future would damage them psychologically or get them into trouble with the law or scupper their job and promotion prospects? This is irrespective of their own personal views on racism. It is my serious submission that racist parents have no moral right to develop in their children ideas and views that would create challenges for the children when they become adults. For as the child matures with the wrong ideas and views on life, unless exceptional circumstances intervene, his racist attitudes would also mature. This will inexorably cause him many problems. So the son, possibly in prison for a proven racist remark or behaviour in public, might not he be justified on reflection to ask himself why his parents had landed him in his predicament? We are here for the purposes of argument, ignoring the effects and results of the alleged racist statement or behaviour on the victim.

The economic effects of racism on the perpetrators, over a long period, are visible and quantifiable. But the psychological damage that the ideology does to them, although not easily discernible, is just as great. For example, if a man, in the privacy of his home gets used to talking and behaving in a racist manner, it is very likely that his children, if he is the traditional stay-in father, will absorb and imbibe his example. The net result is that the boy, perhaps blonde and blue-eyed, with a brilliant mind and hopes of becoming a worthy diplomat of his country, may lose out at an interview, because he was not completely successful in hiding the racist ideas and views instilled in him.

Even if he is lucky to pass the interview and start a career in the foreign service of his country and gets posted to say a country in Asia, Africa, the Pacific Region or the Caribbean, he may one day say or act in a way that may be deemed racist by the host country. A potentially brillliant career with latent ambassadorial prospects would thus come crushing down, following recall home of the unlucky diplomat. And who is to blame for his tragedy?

Let's take another example of the deleterious effects of racism on the racist. The developed countries, all Caucasian except Japan, spend billions of dollars annually at their embassies and consulates promoting good relations with the people of the countries through massive expenditure on cultural programmes, entertainment including extravagant lunches and dinners and cocktail parties and other one-to-one tete-a-tete interactions. All these expensive programmes and activities have a purpose. To make friends and influence people on behalf of and for the benefit of their countries. Altruism has little or no role in the costly exercise.

In the midst of all such noble and patriotic activities, a public statement by a leading academic or politician or writer to the effect that people in those countries in which the diplomats are beavering away are stupid or should be treated as second class human beings because they are not white. Such a statement would completely nullify to a considerable degree the good work of the diplomats. In really serious cases, given global media attention, the ambassador may be called in to the foreign office to explain the stupid, false and unhelpful statement that has gone viral.

Is it right and in the national interest for a single journalist or academic or public figure to birsmirch the name of the whole country of which he is a citizen, all because he wants to sell his book or story? Even more galling is that the offending statement or book is not only racist but based on falsehood and untruths, masquerading as expert opinon or pristine intellectual work.

Examine the case of a business man or corporation which has spent vast sums of money negotiating a diamond or gold or gas and oil concession in a part of the world inhabited by nonwhite people. And ironically these countries constitute about 85% of the world's population and by number of countries, about 75 percent of the global total of seven billion. The discrepancy in the two figures is due to Europe being split into numerous countries, although the total population and areas are quite small, compared with Africa and Asia and the Pacific.

If after all their strenuous and expensive efforts the white investors are stopped in their tracks by a racist statement, book or movie by one or some of their own compatriots, then it can be imagined the colossal harm and damage that the alleged racists have done to their fellow citizens. They have by their single racist act blown away millions of dollars of funds belonging to their country or fellow citizens. For if the exploration, negotiations or other economic activities had succeeded they would have benefitted the economy of their country, through the creation of more jobs, improved exports and improved quality of life for at least a few hundred people. So the offending statement, movie or book, if it is serious enough to affect the white people and the black or non-whites, would destroy jobs not only for the black people but also for the white. And for causing such economic damage the culprits may in certain countries be accused and prosecuted for sabotaging or damaging the national economy or interest. I deem it grossly unfair and unpatriotic for, let's say, an obscure academic, avid for the oxygen of publicity or to satisfy his ego, to bring out a book or statement that puts at risk the hard earned life savings of some of his white compatriots who have invested in the project or business being negotiated for or in operation in Africa, Asia or the Middle East.

It is natural for white racists or their apologists or closet racists to argue that it is a gross infringement on the human rights of the individual or citizen to limit his Freedom of Speech by the state, as personified by the government of the day or by any individual or group. Whilst indeed, freedom of speech is one of the fundamental freedoms in a democracy and true that every person is entitled to his human rights, those who use this line of argument to justify or excuse racism are wrong for the following reasons:

1. The statements of white racists are deeply offensive to their fellow citizens who are black and have the same human rights as their fellow citizens (by birth or naturalization) who are not white or not of European origins. So the racists, in effect by exercising their human rights as they do, are grossly infringing the human rights of their compatriots of a different skin color. The fact that the victim of racism is a visitor or resident and not a citizen, is immaterial. For the law when it comes to trial or sentencing makes no difference between the citizen, visitor, legal or illegal resident. All people are presumed to be equal before the law.

2. Given that the free exercise of human rights is vital for the development and advancement of mankind, to argue that there should be no limits on this freedom would lead to complete anarchy. For if those who argue or maintain that free expression of human rights includes racist comments and insults on others then logically the victims if they have the power would exercise their human rights to rebut or nullify or neutralize their tormentors. For centuries the victims have been in no position whatsoever to counteract the activities, verbal and physical, of the racists. But following the decolonization of Asia, Africa, the Caribbean Islands and the Pacific region, and as the peoples in these areas of the world become more and better

organized, educated and industrialized they would inevitably be in a stronger position to confront their detractors.

It may be noted that racist remarks and activities are almost extinct in the former European colonies, why? The reason is simple. Without the power of a colonial force to implement and support them racists know too well that it would be very unwise to go to any of these countries and talk or behave or act in any way or manner that is deemed racist. The consequences can at best be a strong reprimand and warning by the magistrate. But at worst could be a hefty fine or even a prison sentence. And as one who has been in an African prison for fifteen months, I strongly advise others to avoid that experience. For there are no lovely breakfast and meals, color television, library, comfortable beds and telephone facilities as exist in Western correctional facilities.

In other words, moral considerations apart, and excluding the effects of racism on the victims, it is simply unwise for a white racist to venture outside Europe, still carrying the blight of racism. And as pointed out earlier even in Europe and America, the dynamics of globalization of the economy and the overall effects of intercontinental media operations have made it increasingly rather risky to overtly espouse racist sentiments or exhibit such behavior. So it is not in the best interest of white racists to refuse to lay down the burden of racism, in their own countries or worse, outside their home countries.

Even the most powerful head of state or president or king cannot afford to indulge in the absolute exercise of his human rights or other freedoms. Sadly, the history of Europe, and lately of Africa and Asia, is replete with stories of leaders who believing they had absolute right to give maximum vent to their human rights ended up losing their power or empire. The fortunate ones only lost their power and wealth, and some less lucky sadly lost their heads, which is completely unnecessary and avoidable, in my humble view.

This being the realistic situation, namely that even the most powerful cannot afford to indulge in the absolute enjoyment of their human rights, then the ordinary man, not being in an exalted position, can afford even less to go the whole hog in the realm of human rights.

For he is bereft of the huge power and authority which the president, or head of state has accrued through free and fair elections or by force of arms or by organized threat of force.

Interestingly, just as when the president or head of state has no or few friends and supporters, if he falls, so the racist will have no allies when the consequences of his statement or behaviour attract public attention and condemnation. Even his family and friends may join in his condemnation. Privately they may continue to harbor identical views as their beleaguered compatriot in trouble, but not in public!

Finally it needs be stated that on the issue of the role of human rights as it affects racism, excluding the harm and damage to the victim, the perpetrator also suffers. Let's take the example of a prominent highly educated man or rich man or high profile personality who in fully exercising his human rights at home gets used to frequently talking or behaving in a racist manner. As pointed out earlier, his actions give a very bad example to his children who naturally are likely to absorb and imbibe his pattern of speech and behavior. They are therefore likely to get into trouble either at home in their own country or worse if they are abroad.

The other casualty of the behavior of the father is ironically the man himself. For used to his unbridled racist talk or behavior, as he is, there is a great possibility that one day, unguardedly or unwittingly or in a very brief moment of forgetfulness, careless talk or behavior in public will be deemed racist by those round him or the media. This is in spite of all his determined efforts to adopt a nonracist persona once outside his home. Should such an episode befall him, who would he have to blame for his loss of prestige, loss of face, money and other assets? In these days of evolving sophisticated mobile phones, secret cameras and other devices that can easily capture on record statements and actions, it becomes very unwise, moral considerations apart, for the racist to develop the habit of giving free rein to his racism, through the exercise of his human rights. Regularly and frequently the media, especially in the United States Of America, the BBC, and the Arab television station ALJAZEERA, publicize major stories of high profile men and personalities who have lost jobs, personal esteem or considerable money as a result of their own racism. Such self-inflicted harm and injury, I submit can easily be painlessly avoided.

So even the white people who are not racists but aid and abet the activities of their racist fellow citizens or turn a blind eye to what they are saying or have deaf ears to their statements should realize that they are doing their compatriots immense harm by cheering them on or giving vicarious support to their actions or statements through their silence. Ironically the harm that the racists do themselves tends to spill over to those who may indeed abhor their reprehensible behavior or statements.

If, let's say, the wife of a rabid racist continues to ignore the racist rantings at home of her husband and makes no serious effort to help him free himself from the psychological burden that he is carrying, should she be surprised when on a bright afternoon she gets a call from the local police that her husband has been arrested for gross racist remarks or behavior and that he needs her as a matter of urgency at the police station?

It is my submission that at the very least the stress and trauma that the wife has to endure following the call could surely have been avoided if she had initially tried to tone down her husband's behavior or rhetoric or done her best to ensure that his pattern of speech or behavior was limited to the confines of their home. For inside their home, which metaphorically speaking is their castle, a man indeed has the right to think and talk and behave as he wishes but outside he loses some of that freedom, even in the most democratic and liberal society on earth.

To argue that the man or for that matter any person, of whatever race or skin color should be allowed or be free to say or do what he likes or fancies is in effect giving oxygen to a life of anarchy, in which all suffer. Indeed it is for good reason that our ancestors thousands of years ago, starting as naked, roaming human beings, although the highest forms of animals, gradually for survival reasons developed clothing. It became a vital necessity against the elements, particularly in the cold climates. Subsequently, aesthetic considerations led to improvements in quality and designs of clothing, but the original need remained the same.

The stage has been reached for the past few millennia where it is obligatory in any civilized society for people to go about wearing clothes, irrespective of the weather conditions or their fervent desire to go about naked. The freedom, available to Homo sapiens many millennia ago, has been drastically whittled down and any person who insists on exercising their desire to go naked would be sanctioned or stopped from doing so. Of course, if it is established after a psychiatric evaluation that the person is not well, then he or she would receive appropriate medical attention and care.

Another example of a restriction on 'human rights' which is established and accepted in all countries, including even the least developed countries may be considered here. Although urinating is a normal and indeed a vital physiological function for all animals, including human beings, all countries have strict laws prohibiting it in public. The law is not against urinating per se, but against doing so in a public place, because over the hundreds of years, certainly from the eighteenth century, human beings have learnt that such an activity, although essential and vital for good health and wellbeing, if done in public spreads pathogenic bacteria and viruses which cause diseases to humans, including the perpetrators of such acts.

Indeed, the other reason for such a ban, namely that urinating in public offends the sensibilities of others and debases the dignity of the human being is a minor factor in the initiation and implementation of such a limitation on human rights.

The person who wants to exercise his human right to pollute the environment poses a health risk not only to himself but also to others. And who gives him the right to endanger the lives of his fellow humans? Furthermore, just as in a civilized society a person cannot go about naked in public and would be stopped from so doing, because his nakedness is offensive to others likewise, any effort to display one's nakedness in public, albeit partly by urinating would and must be prevented or stopped. For again no man is entitled in the advancement of his human rights to offend the sensibilities of his fellow human beings. Thus any effort to so do is in effect a significant blow to the human rights of others.

We may also consider another infringement on human rights or individual freedom in recent years, which even now in the twenty first century some libertarians are not happy about. Right up to the 1960's cigarette smoking was fashionable in Europe and America. Indeed, the more expensive the cigarettes and the accompanying holders, the greater the social esteem of the smoker. Then in 1963, after much medical research in Europe and the United States, it was established conclusively that the habit caused lung cancer, heart disease, high blood pressure and other cardiovascular complaints and illnesses. So, starting with the United States of America, governments in the developed countries passed laws banning the smoking of cigarettes in public places such as hotels, restaurants, halls, shops and other public venues. This was a major attack on individual freedom or human rights, namely the right of a person to smoke if even it harms him, despite the cost.

This major diminution of human rights for the common good, following fierce opposition by some smokers and others, has come to be accepted by and large. For the wisdom in the law restricting human rights is apparent and clear for the following reasons: First, the smoke affects primarily the smoker and secondarily those near him. Two, if the smoker is determined to risk or undermine his health, he has no right whatsoever to endanger others without their permission. Three, by his action he is creating a health problem for his compatriots who have to pay taxes to look after him when his self-induced illness occurs. Four, assuming that the smoker wishes to die early through the exercise of his human right or freedom to smoke knowing that it will result in his early demise, is it his right to deprive his relatives and friends of his company by such an untimely death? Finally, what about the financial investment of his fellow citizens in his education, growth, development and welfare, in expectation that he would live a reasonably long life making a meaningful contribution to the welfare and progress of his compatriots and humanity at large?

So the infringement or reduction in his human rights trumps his desire to demand his freedom as a human being. Fortunately in most countries of the world, including many of the developing countries, the rationale for banning smoking in public is accepted as reasonable and pragmatic. Of course, there are millions of people the world over who still feel or maintain that their human rights are, or should be, paramount. Smoking harms the individual and those around him, his family and his country, just as Racism does. But the worst victim from racism in the long run is the racist himself, with collateral damage to his children and grandchildren. Why should racists leave a huge negative legacy for their offspring to deal with as sadly is happening in South Africa now?

# CHAPTER 9

# ERADICATION OF RACISM AT THE INTERNATIONAL LEVEL

The United Nations organization, which since its establishment in 1946 has passed important resolutions against racism, is in my view a good example of what a good employer should be when it comes to employment practices. For although initially most of the personnel were white, over the years this situation has changed dramatically. That originally at its inception it was an all-white body should come as no surprise. For apart from the Chinese all the founding members were white, who initiated the idea of setting up the main international post war organization to promote peace, development and stability worldwide, having learnt from the horrendous experiences of the Second World War. In any case as all the countries in Asia, Africa and the Pacific region were colonies of the European nations they could not be members of the august organization.

Despite the fact that the contributions from some countries, based on their Gross Domestic Product, population and other factors are tiny, a fair proportion of their nationals are in the employment of the United Nations. As the United States alone pays at least 22% and more towards the funding of the organization, it means that if the level of national contributions was to be the only criterion for employment then that country alone could claim about 25% of the employment positions. Also, if qualifications, competence and merit alone were to be the yardstick for filling the positions then surely even the State of Illinois alone or the city of London easily could muster enough suitably qualified men and women to fill all the positions available. But such a situation would not appropriately reflect the whole ethos of the United Nations as a world body, encompassing all geographical regions, races and religions.

So it is right and proper that fairness and regional representation are also factors to determine the composition of the staffing of the world organization at various levels of employment. For if the body with a global reach and influence were to be manned by Caucasians, ignoring the rest of the peoples of the world who constitute about 85 percent of the population then the organization would not be living up to its claim as a global body meant for all peoples, irrespective of race, creed or color. By passing resolutions condemning racism and encouraging members to abide by them, the United Nations has established a bench mark by which its members can be evaluated on the important issue of racism.

All the agencies of the United Nations such as the International Atomic Energy Agency, World Health Organization, UNESCO and the World Food Program, do indeed reflect their global reach, objective and activities through the multinational composition of their work force. Admittedly, the figures vary among the organizations but it is safe to state that their multinational composition cannot be disputed. Thus the United Nations, as the supreme world organization, has not only passed resolutions against racism but has also set a noble example for other international bodies, which claim to operate globally and be responsible for the welfare of all peoples within their remit to follow suit. For if international bodies and organizations are seen or perceived as being predominantly white enclaves then their international credentials become flawed, even if the justification for the anomaly is that merit, competence and qualifications are the only criteria that they consider in their employment procedures.

With the noble example set by the United Nations Organization it is hoped that other great charitable organizations like Amnesty International, the Red Cross, Doctors Without Borders and other affiliates of the United Nations would emulate the shining work evidenced by the recruitment and promotion procedures of the United Nations. Otherwise they risk being seen or perceived as not doing enough to combat or eradicate racism. Naturally as all these organizations and similar bodies were initiated and established by white people, it is not surprising that initially, practically all the staff and employees, especially at the higher echelons of power, were white.

However, with the dramatic increase in the numbers of educated and competent men and women in Asia and Africa, the old argument that there were not sufficient numbers of Asian and Africans to fill certain positions become vacuous and untenable. Additionally, if these august and highly respected organizations, which are looked up to by hundreds of millions of people do not want or cannot set a good example in multiracial harmony and coexistence then they considerably diminish their moral right and authority as global bodies.

There is also the psychological factor that strengthens the need for the various world bodies to reflect as much as practically possible the major regions of the world. For example, if an international tribunal trying an African leader accused of genocide has a black judge on the panel, of course duly qualified, the accused has little cause to claim that say a long sentence of imprisonment was so given to him because all the judges, prosecutors, and court staff were white. It is not here suggested that an all-white tribunal cannot deliver a fair verdict. Far from it. What is postulated here is that human nature being what it is, the verdict and sentence would look far fairer in the eyes of many people, black and white, and including the accused, if among the panel of judges is another nonwhite person. For justice must not only be done but be seen to be done!

After all, the principle of equity and fairness is incorporated in the selection of juries in all the developed countries and in many of the developing countries also. Say in a trial of a man accused of rape, if both men and women serve on the jury, the convicted person can hardly complain that the verdict was gender-biased. For wouldn't he have a plausible cause for complaint if all the jurors were female plus a female prosecutor, court staff and psychologist, however overwhelming the evidence against him? Thus in respect of the world bodies mentioned above, it is very important that they show by not only words but also by deeds, that they abhor and repudiate racism by demonstrating that their workforce, particularly in control and command positions, are truly reflective of the world that they claim to represent and serve. Otherwise they lose their moral right to call themselves international bodies serving the whole of humanity and not only people of European extraction or race.

Toward their proclaimed credentials as global organizations, it is only right and proper and evidence of good administration if any of their staff are proven to be engaging in racist talk or behavior that such miscreants are not only exposed but disciplined appropriately. By so doing the leaders of the said organizations are primarily doing their institutions much favor through upholding their good name globally.

Secondly, immediate and firm disciplinary action against employees who want or are tempted to soil the name of their institutions are saved from the danger and risk of a repetition of such untoward behavior which in some countries might earn them not only loss of office but possibly a stiff fine or even imprisonment. So from the perspective of an educated, impartial, well-meaning African or Asian, men and women in powerful leadership positions in world bodies who wittingly or unwittingly try to cover the racist activities or speech of their employees or colleagues of similar rank are, forgetting about the Asian and African victims, in reality doing their colleagues immense harm.

As the resolutions by the United Nations on Racism are binding on all member countries they apply or should apply with even greater force on the agencies and bodies that operate under the umbrella of the august organization itself. And even where an international body is not directly under the United Nations or affiliated to it or funded by it, fully or partly, they cannot afford to ignore the moral imperative of such resolutions. That is if they expect to be taken seriously as highly esteemed institutions with a global reach and mandate.

It is therefore encouraging and commendable that in recent years the international football federation (FIFA), has publicly been seen to take a firm and robust action against football teams or fans that have brought the great game into disrepute by either their public utterances or behavior. As football is played in all countries from the hottest desolate desert areas to the coldest regions of the globe, it is right and proper that owners, managers or trainers do not connive and condone racism by turning a blind eye or deaf ear to untoward public statements or actions, especially when they emanate from high profile people or from people with responsible positions in society.

For by doing so, their unethical and unprofessional stance would only go to harm the racist perpetrators. In that, used to their racist statements and actions going unchallenged, such unfortunate people may one day repeat similar statements or behavior in places that would cause them enormous loss or embarrassment or even imprisonment. So in reality people in positions of authority in sport who do not take firm disciplinary actions against racism are doing their fellow citizens immense harm. Of course, with a sense of misguided loyalty they may think that they are doing their erring friends a great favor. Surely, a man who observes his close friend engaging gaily in a social activity of a high risk health hazard and does not endeavor to persuade his friend to stop cannot be said to be a good and true friend!

So although it is very important that wherever and whenever racism shows its ugly head FIFA take prompt action, even more important is the need to place in position mechanisms and programs to prevent such occurrences. For example many sports bodies in many countries in the Americas and Europe have launched public programs to ensure that fans, managers, promoters and players all get the message, loud and clear, that racism in sports or on their fields is wrong and unacceptable. And that those found talking or behaving in a racist manner would pay a high price for their actions.

Until the programs or campaigns to eradicate racism begin to emphasize the consequences to people or organizations of their actions, little progress will be made. To date even the most enlightened anti-racist activities or programs have tended to overemphasize or dwell on the harm to the victims. Sadly, we do not live in an ideal world where all human beings do the right thing for altruistic reasons. In practically all cases, most people desist from saying or doing what they would like because of the consequences that are likely or certain to flow from their actions and where the consequences would be unpalatable or negative, the deterrent acts well for the benefit of mankind. Of course, here excluded are dare-devil criminals and diehards. But even these have been known to attempt avoiding the direct legal results of their actions or statements by either fleeing, hiding or hiring expensive lawyers to bail or free them or by resorting to diverse strategies to nullify in their favor, the Law of Karma or Newton's Third Law of Motion. In a flash of amnesia they forget that the laws are immutable and do apply to all of us, including them. From moral dereliction, there is no escape!

The firm and unambiguous stand against racism that was taken in April 2014 in the United States of America by the NBA authorities when proven evidence of racism was brought to their attention is a classic example of what those in command and control positions in sports and allied fields can do to eradicate this scourge. By their prompt and firm action the authorities set a good example for similar bodies to emulate. People all over the world who watched the unfolding of the Donald Sterling race saga or read about it saw for themselves that it is becoming increasingly disadvantageous to indulge in racism. For although the gentleman in question did later offer a full public apology for what he called 'a terrible mistake', the financial, psychological and other damage to him must have been at the very least quite considerable.

For the benefit of readers who perhaps might have missed the story in question, I here give it in outline. In April 2014 the world media reported that a gentleman by name Donald Sterling, who was the owner of the Los Angeles Clippers professional basketball franchise of the national basketball association (NBA) from 1981 – 2014, had been found to be making racist comments after private recordings had been made public. Although he made a public apology and denying he is a racist, he was fined 2.5 million dollars, the maximum fine allowed by the NBA constitution, and banned from the NBA for life. His wife Shelly Sterling made a deal to sell the Clippers for 2 billion dollars to a Steve Balmer, and although they still came out with a huge amount of money, just a slip of the tongue on a private recording was still a terrible mistake which cost Donald Sterling his franchise and millions of dollars. It is my firm belief that this tragedy was completely avoidable.

The United Nations Declaration of Human Rights passed in 1948 to which all nations subscribe clearly denounces and condemns racism. As such, governments of member states of the revered global body who do not ensure that the letter and spirit of the declaration are seriously and firmly implemented in their countries are not only doing a dis-service to their countries and people but also bringing the world body to ridicule. For if the resolutions and directives of the United Nations are ignored or flouted with impunity, then the moral and legal authority of the organization is diminished. This is especially so if the said UN declarations and resolutions are violated by the countries which by virtue of their historic associations with the UN as founding members or by the levels of their UN contributions, exert immense influence on the international body. And all these countries, barring a couple, are European or of European extraction.

For Africans and Asians and other non-Europeans from the Caribbean Islands, Pacific Region and South America, it is encouraging and uplifting to observe in recent years a growing presence of their people in high profile positions and in global assignments. However, it is submitted here that positive as this trend is, more could be done to accelerate the process. In doing so, the United Nations would be dealing a heavy blow against racism and also prodding its members to do likewise. As the United Nations is a unique world body, which is looked up to by hundreds of millions of people, what the organization does, by word or deed, has profound influence and consequences beyond its halls and corridors of power. Thus if most of its agencies or committees or delegations are staffed by white people, the impression would be given that there are not sufficient numbers of suitably qualified and experienced personnel from the countries populated by non-Europeans.

Such a stance would not only be incorrect and untrue but would effectively be giving life to racism, when it rather should be dying from the face of the earth. With certain countries in Africa and Asia having large pools of highly educated, fair-minded, decent experienced and first class administrators and experts of various types, any defense of insufficient representation of Africans and Asians at all levels of the great world body becomes untenable and unacceptable. It only plays into the hands of racists at the time in human history when the writing is clearly on the wall that this human scourge which has done so much harm to so many peoples for so long is on its last legs.

As most international bodies and charities, for example the Red Cross, Amnesty International, Food Aid, Water Aid and Fair Trade were founded by white people, their contributions towards the cause of anti-racism can be enormous. This can be done firstly by being seen to adopt programs and activities that are manifestly against racism. Secondly with all the victims of racism being in Asia, Africa and the Caribbean and Pacific regions, the international organizations should, in furtherance of the eradication of racism, initiate and promote programs that raise the levels of education and health in the underdeveloped countries. For one of the major justifications for racism, albeit not always expressed openly by racists, is the wide gap in education between countries where many of the people are illiterate and those which are literate. And using the levels of education as a measure of intelligence, racists have concluded for at least four centuries that the illiterate and uneducated are 'stupid and inferior' to them.

Support for this view is shown by the rapid changes in attitudes by white racists towards Japan. Up till the middle of the twentieth century, negative and uncomplimentary statements, comments and behavior towards Japan and the Japanese people by white racists were quite common in Europe and America. But with the rapid development of Japan in the fields of education, science, engineering, robotics, technology and industry, any claim by white racists of racial superiority became less and less tenable and more and more laughable and ridiculous. Indeed, from 1979 to 2010, a land of only 128 million people, Japan was the largest economy in the whole world, surpassed by the United States of America, with a population of 317 million.

Thus the rapid industrial and economic development of Japan made it increasingly utterly ridiculous for any racist to maintain a stance of superiority, although such a posture ab initio was without any shred of support in science or reason. The consequences of the achievements of Japan, a non- European country, have produced notable effects on the aspirations of millions of people who are not Europeans. For these people have seen for themselves that they can indeed chalk achievements as great as those of white people or even greater, in shorter time and at less cost. The prerequisites for such noble achievements are not skin color or race but education, hard work, good leadership, self-sacrifice, determination and perseverance.

# CHAPTER 10

# THE UNSUNG HEROES AND WARRIORS

In the United Kingdom the fight against racism started as far back as the fifteenth century when the importation of slaves to the country began. As the country was smaller than the United States and as, especially there was no economic need for slaves, few were sent to Great Britain. They mostly ended as servants and labourers. But although racism was in the UK not as vicious and widespread as in America it was still in existence. So the long drawn out struggle against slavery must be seen as part of the fight against racism. The heroic and bold public campaigns against slavery by leaders like William Wilberforce, Charles James Fox and William Roscoe Buxton, led eventually to the abolition in the British Empire by the British Parliament, in 1807. Then in 1834 Parliament banned it in all the colonies.

This milestone in the struggle against slavery was followed by other European nations which were also actively engaged in slavery. Thus the abominable trade was abolished by the Dutch in 1814, by the Germans (Prussia) in 1807 and the Spanish partially abolished slavery of African slaves, except in Cuba, Puerto Rico and Santo Domingo in 1811 and were paid 400,000 English pounds by the British in 1815 to cease slave trading in those colonies. Meanwhile the French, as part of the Revolution of 1789 had proscribed it. But as all these European nations and others, including Portugal and

Italy had colonies in Africa and Asia, it meant that although slavery had been abolished, its mutant form, racism still flourished. For there needed to be a rationale for a practice which to all Christians was manifestly unchristian and ungodly. Especially as all the slave-trading colonial nations were Christians or claimed to be so.

The rationale used to justify this most unchristian of acts was the inferiority of the non-white races because they had not developed steel weapons and all the paraphernalia of sixteenth century European life. This entirely subjective evaluation of the achievements of nonwhite races by white races did not take into account the historic and epoch making achievements of non-Europeans in Africa, South America, the Middle East and Asia by people of non-European origins. Where such notable achievements were acknowledged at all, they were either marginalized or hidden. For to publicize or trumpet these achievements meant in effect undermining and torpedoing the philosophical and religious rationale for racism. So with even religious leaders supporting or condoning or conniving at the inhuman practice of racism, the ideology grew from strength to strength. It was only in the late 1900's that in Britain serious efforts were made at the legislative levels to confront racism. In 1963 the first definite law against racism was passed in UK. This made the practice a criminal offence in public and in the provision of public housing, education and other services.

It therefore became illegal to display openly notices such as 'Room to Let, White Gents only', with some racists adding for full measure, 'No Irish', 'No Jews'. But good and effective as the laws were in gnawing at racism they could not touch the heart and soul of the citizenry where the problem lay. For in a democracy there is a limit to what laws can be passed and despite the establishment of Committees and Commissions charged with ensuring racial equality and the eradication of racism, the problem still has not gone away. Yet it is doing so, little by little, as more and more people, through education, travel, social media and parental direction gradually lose their morbid or perceived threat of the stranger, especially if he is of a different skin color to themselves.

Progress in advancing the cause against racism in Great Britain has come about chiefly as a result of massive public pressure through mass demonstrations, protests and boycotts by the unknown and unsung millions of white people. These mass protests against racism particularly from the mid 1950's, some of them led by eminent scholars, academics and politicians in the country have sent collectively a clear message to their leaders that the time for change had come. The names such as Lord Bertrand Russell(one of Britain's most famous philosophers), Michael Foot, leader of the Labour Party, Reverend Michael Scott, the anti-apartheid activist, Bishop Trevor Huddleston, Tony Benn, an outstanding statesman who gave up his peerage, so as to identify with the populates, Jeremy Thorpe, leader of the Liberal Party, and many others meant that such manifestations of the public will could not be fobbed off as the trouble-making activities of rabble rousers. Also significant and worthy of note was the fact that the preponderant numbers of the demonstrators were white, including thousands of young men and women, sometimes with their babies in prams or on the shoulders of their fathers!!. Yes, they were being taught at a very early age to stand up for what was right.

All these hundreds of thousands of nameless, unknown and unsung people are warriors who have labored to bring racism to the point in the UK, where it is gradually dying. The whole process of change must necessarily be gradual. For if a system, however obnoxious and despicable, has been entrenched in the language, literature, customs and traditions of a people, well embedded in their psyche, it is rather naïve and unrealistic to expect root-stem-and branch change overnight. So it is the right thing to do for all victims of racism and all others who genuinely believe in the equality of mankind and in democracy, to give praise and honor to those who have made their modest contributions to ridding the world of racism. That many of the young white men and women participating in the anti-racism demonstrations were the sons and daughters of law makers in their country could not but have dwelt on the minds of their parents and their friends. As the only African journalist in

London in those hectic days of mass demonstrations in the late 1950's early 1960's against apartheid and racism, I could not but be struck by the fact that the overwhelming numbers of the participants were European!.

Admittedly, in all the other European countries where racism has existed, as an appendage of colonialism there have indeed been in recent years, from the 1950's, public protests by many white people against racism. There is no disputing this! But equally significant has been the fact that the import and scale of the mass protests in America and the United Kingdom have acted as catalysts for similar movements in countries where racism is rife. Interestingly, the two nations that have been most actively involved in slavery and racism are also the same countries that have been in the forefront of the fight to rid the world of those twin evils. Thus whilst not marginalizing the effects of such movements in Australia, New Zealand, Europe and Canada, it is safe to state that both the United States of America and the United Kingdom have in recent years been in the fore front of the struggle against racism.

Especially commendable has been the bold principled stance of the Scandinavian countries. At the apogee of racism in South Africa, enshrined and personified in Apartheid, there were not only massive demonstrations and rallies in these countries, but also their governments gave financial and other forms of support to the anti-apartheid campaigns and the victims of racism. Little wonder that Nelson Mandela, after his release from 26 years of imprisonment for anti-apartheid activities paid his first overseas visit to these countries.

I am of the considered view that in America, Europe and in parts of the world, where racism has been in existence for centuries, monuments should be built or set up for the thousands of white people who in the struggle against racism suffered severely or even lost their lives. In memorializing them, their compatriots would be showing gratitude for their moral stand and immense foresight. Such publicly visible monuments would also serve the purpose of limiting the damage which can be done by many Asians and Africans who are tempted or inclined to lump all Caucasians together as racist.

For I am of the conviction that as a result of the centuries of racism by white people against nonwhite nonwhites, sometimes very brutal and inhuman, especially in their colonies, there is a tendency for the victims to forget or marginalise the stupendous efforts of millions of white people in the eradication of racism. Any serious effort to debate or discuss racism intended to hasten its demise must take a holistic approach to the problem. And in doing so must set the record straight by acknowledging the noble role played by people who were or are not the victims of racism themselves.

This modest work on racism would be incomplete without placing on record the enormous contributions of the millions of Europeans and Americans since the days of slavery who have resolutely and boldly stood up against racism. They have done so in spite of bitter name-calling, verbal abuse and sometimes even physical assault. These are white men and women who knew and felt that the system of slavery and its underpinning ideology of racism was immoral.

The nobility of the stance of these great people is enhanced by the fact that as white men and women themselves they were beneficiaries, directly or indirectly, from the very system that they were robustly attacking and wanted to eliminate. To put ethical considerations over and above financial or economic interests is most admirable and the actions of those people over many decades do, in my humble opinion, make up considerably for the evil and inhuman activities of their fellow compatriots

It may be argued that those who supported slavery and racism, and still do, are blameless because they did not know that what they were doing was evil and wrong, but I do not think so. I firmly believe that human beings who indulge or participate in racism, or slavery, past or present know, in their hearts, that what they are doing is wrong. Ultimately, it is a moral issue: Would they like done to themselves what they were doing to their victims?

In the four centuries from the fifteenth to the nineteenth, when slavery was abolished, these noble and selfless people in Europe and the Americas worked valiantly against slavery. In America, the most memorable name is that of President Abraham Lincoln, who will forever be remembered. In pursuit of the principle that slavery was wrong, he led a war to convince his compatriots that it must end.

The Civil Rights Act and the Voting Rights Act of 1963 and 1964 are to the credit of Dr. Martin Luther King who by mobilising and galvanizing the generality of the population, created the political environment that led to the passing of both laws by Congress and quickened the tempo of the drive against racism in America. However, to the extent that the Congress was almost completely white, the legislation does credit to the nation. President Johnson, a Democrat was in office then. Six Republican Senators voted against the legislation. Twenty one Democrat Senators voted against it.

Apart from legislative action by Congress over the decades individual American Presidents have publicly registered their opposition to racism by certain specific individual actions. For example, in 1953, Mr. Komla Gbedemah, secretary of the Treasury of the Gold Coast (after independence in 1957 called Ghana) was on a visit to the USA and went to a restaurant near the White House for a meal where he was turned away. The story was well published in the US and other foreign media, particularly by the BBC. The following day the President of the US, President Dwight Eisenhower, invited the humiliated Ghanaian government minister to the White House for breakfast. The significance of this noble presidential stance against racism was not lost on the public, nor on hundreds of millions of white people in Europe, Africa, and the Asia-Pacific region.

The integration of the US armed forces in 1948 by President Harry Truman was one of the greatest achievements of his tenure. For it was a trail-blazer in the integration of not only the armed forces, but also the federal employee system. Many eminent African Americans came to public prominence during the second half of the twentieth century. John Harold Johnson, the iconic African American businessman and publisher of Ebony magazine, was the first African-American to appear in Forbes 400. According to Wikipedia, Johnson was invited by the US government to participate in several international missions. In August 1976 he devoted an entire issue of Ebony to 'Africa, the

Continent of the Future' and in 1996, President Clinton bestowed on him the Presidential Medal of Freedom for his work against racism and for his promotion of the dignity of the black man.

The Civil Rights legislation did not overnight eradicate racism in America, but it dealt major blows to the abhorrent ideology. Furthermore, America's example gave clear notice to other peoples of European origin or extraction, be they in Europe itself or in Australia, South Africa or New Zealand, that the richest and most powerful nation in the world was actively disengaging from its racist past and present.

Off course we cannot in any way ignore the herculean efforts of brave African-Americans who for several decades, at the risk of even their lives campaigned openly against racism, institutional and otherwise. Right from the dark days of slavery, there have been men and women of colour who at the risk of having their churches or houses torched have fearlessly stood up to be counted and robustly contributed to the fight against slavery and its underpinning ideology of racism. Their heroic work speaks for itself and is deservedly recorded in the annals of history. But at this point, I am highlighting the supreme efforts of courageous white people who, on altruistic and moral grounds, stood up for what was right, despite the (incorrect) assumption by many that racism promoted the economic interests of the whites.

The hundreds of missionaries from America who went voluntarily to South America, Africa and Asia, risking inclement weather and adverse environmental conditions, apart from spreading Christianity, also sowed and nurtured the seeds of education, which have grown to empower the local people and made them less prone to the physical and psychological ravages of racism.

Additionally, millions of white men and women, particularly students have for several years participated actively in the fight against racism. They have done this through taking part in mass public marches, sit-ins and boycotts of shops or institutions notorious for their racism. And consistently, the results of these mass movements have been the same. After initial resistance or opposition, sometimes even violence, the racists have given in reluctantly or have been overcome. For their cause is morally indefensible and as increasing numbers of their fellow citizens become less bigoted, travel more or adopt a rational attitude to the whole phenomenon of racism, and its negative impact on their jobs, families and their own reputations, they eventually join those who are not racists.

However, it is in recent years that the most significant advances have been made in the fight against racism. All the major employers and corporations have effective and active equal opportunities or anti–racism programs to ensure that from board directors down to the lowest level, nothing is said or done (at least not in public !) which can be interpreted or construed as racist, thus causing unnecessary and unwelcome publicity and financial damages to the employers or corporations concerned. Altruistic or moral considerations apart, this public stance against racism makes eminent sense. For the courts hand down very heavy fines and damages against institutions, corporations or individuals who, after trial are found guilty of hate or race-related crimes. The desire, therefore of many individuals or organizations, mired in such cases to seek out of court settlements is perfectly understandable.

The historic integration of the United States armed forces by President Harry S. Truman paved the way for a swathe of societal changes for the better. It also led to the advancement of thousands of African-American officers. For once promotion and recognition were based purely on merit, and not skin colour, it became apparent that non-white soldiers or officers were as capable, brave and competent as their white comrades. The epochal program of racial integration in the US armed forces started in 1948 was to culminate in the appointment in October, 1989 (under the administration of President G H Bush) of General Colin Powell as the first Afro-American chairman of the Joint Chiefs of Staff (overall head) of the US armed forces.

This in effect made him head of not only the most powerful military in the whole world, but also head of the military forces in the non-communist Western world. He had previously been head of the army (the first nonwhite). In 2001, he was appointed Secretary of State by President George Bush. In 2005, President Bush next appointed African-American woman, Dr. Condolezza Rice as Secretary of State, in a country overwhelmingly white. This goes to show that, indeed, where there is the will, there is a way! These historic appointments and others have been made in spite of any stiff opposition.

President Dwight D. Eisenhower carried further the process of eradicating racism in America by sending in federal troops to Little Rock, Arkansas, to enforce the integration of schools and buses which had been mandated by a court order. It was a major and significant onslaught on racism, with immense repercussions and reverberations through the country and beyond.

The struggle against racism was carried further by President John F. Kennedy with the establishment of the Peace Corps in 1961. The epochal work of the thousands of American young men and women voluntarily spending two or three years of their lives working in most inclement conditions in the far flung corners of the world will ever remain one of the greatest contributions of the United States of America to the cause of human progress. All their fantastic work was in the developing countries of the world, where the people are non-Caucasian. Admittedly a few of the volunteers were African-American but indisputably, the overwhelming majority were white.

I wish to digress and add a personal note here. When we lived in Accra, Ghana's capital, we always made it a point to stop our car and give a ride to those volunteers that we saw walking on the road side in the hot, humid sun. Many of them had hideous marks of mosquito bites on their skin. Taking them home and enjoying a meal with them and sometimes a swim in the pool, we could not but admire their sincere friendliness and genuine efforts to help other human beings who suffered. Their fervent enthusiasm to devote a part of their lives serving the underprivileged, deprived, ignorant and sick was inspirational. So for me as a writer, in joining the millions of voices world-wide against racism, I cannot fail to put on record the great and noble work of millions of white people who have stood up against racism, despite vilification, name-calling, insults and even sometimes physical assaults from their fellow white people. For whilst the monumental work that has been achieved by black leaders in America to eradicate racism is admirable, such efforts and work assume superhuman significance, when emanating from white people and their leaders. For by their actions they make morality trump present economic and social privilege.

The thousands of white American missionaries who travelled to remote corners of South America, Africa and Asia spreading Christianity have by taking knowledge to unfortunate peoples, empowered them and their children and grandchildren to resist the devastating blows of racism. As the old adage goes, 'Knowledge is Power'. Therefore, he who spreads knowledge, or advances its cause, promotes empowerment. This ultimately leads inexorably to the reduction in racism. As people become more and more educated they are less and less likely to indulge in racism, whilst contemporaneously the victims of racism, newly empowered are better fortified to withstand the physical and psychological effects of the inhuman ideology which is the antithesis of what all the major religions cherish and advocate.

When President George Bush Jr, appointed Dr. Condolezza Rice to be the first African-American woman Secretary of State, he was effectively following the noble path in the struggle against racism, with its history stretching back over many decades.

The fight against the evil and shortsighted ideology and practice of racism was carried to unbelievable lengths when in 2008, the voters in America in free and fair elections, open to all adults, voluntarily elected the first black president of the country. Although President Barack Obama is biracial with a white American mother and Kenyan father, and therefore is neither black nor white, the conventional concensus is that he is labelled black, and identifies himself as black. It is therefore very significant and noteworthy that in a predominantly white voting public, he won. It demonstrates the determination of the voters, especially among the youth, to ignore skin color as a negative criterion for selection of a President. On the contrary, by electing Obama as President, the American voters sent a strong message that they can no longer be characterized as racist!

His second victory, with an even increased number of votes showed that the first victory was not a fluke but indicated a sea-change in the American public where multi-culturalism and the rejection of racism had at last become main-stream. For by the time of the second election the voters had been able to judge President Barack Obama by his liberal record and they gave him a resounding victory. Again, as before his challenger was white. What both victories signify is that although racism is not dead in America, step by step, little by little, poco a poco, more and more white people in their millions have demonstrably taken a robust stand against it.

I have no wish to insinuate that all those who did not vote for Obama were racist, as not everyone agreed with his policies, but that is beyond the scope of this book. The fact remains that whether despite, or because of his skin colour, the American public voted for a black President and that fact alone has changed America for the better and given a shining example to the world that a nation can indeed overcome its shameful past.

The greatness and monumental import of what the American electorate did in electing President Obama as their country's leader and thus leader of the West and its allies and friends, takes on a gargantuan dimension when it is remembered that his opponent in the election was a famous, greatly respected senator, a celebrated war veteran to cap it all. The significance of his victory and election could not have been lost on fellow white citizens.

The historic election victories of President Barack Obama, although they did not end racism in America, demonstrated that the overwhelming majority of white people in the country are prepared and welcome change for the better in race relations. For as it is still an advantage to be white in America, Canada, parts of South America, Europe, Australia and New Zealand white people in America and in those countries who, despite the immense advantages that they enjoy because of their race, are yet willing and ready for ethical reasons to rise above these advantages and take up or join the cause of non-whites cannot but be greatly admired for their altruism.

Off course there is possibly an element of long-sightedness, metaphorically speaking in this stance of theirs. For as events in South Africa have shown since the end of Apartheid in 1994 there is always the high probability that those who gleefully indulge or actively participate in racism may end as victims of the very ideology and practices that they have advocated or unabashedly advanced. From this point of view, it becomes apparent that active white racists are in effect the worst enemies of the vast majority, who either are not racists or are only benignly so. For it is highly debatable whether the robust advocates of Apartheid and white supremacy in South Africa over the centuries before 1994 would have taken the stand that they did, had they foreseen the adverse impact it would eventually wreak on their children and grandchildren.

I have deliberately given due attention to the positive developments in race relations in America, for the following reasons. Firstly, the United States of America, as the richest and most powerful nation on earth does have a huge influence on the rest of the world. The repercussions of what transpires there have direct and indirect effects on the rest of humanity. Thus my old friend Congressman Danny Kenyatta Davis was not exaggerating at all when in his inaugural speech at the House of Representatives, he said with flair, that he was honoured to be speaking in the Chamber where laws are made which affect not only the United States of America, but the whole world! Off course, many people would not accept this evaluation of Congressman Danny K. Davis and they are entitled to their opinions. But as the effects and ramifications on the rest of the globe of the financial and economic crisis that began in the United States in 2008 proved, indeed the Congressman was being prescient and not at all hyperbolic or verbose or emotional!

Secondly, as that country, although with only a population of about three hundred and twenty million, (about 4.6% of the world's population of seven thousand million) accounts for 22-25% of the global GDP, any social or political or financial activity that occurs there, simply does not end in the country. No wonder there is an English saying that 'When America sneezes, Europe has a cold!'And would it then be severe flu or pneumonia for countries outside America not so well endowed?. Thus a strong and robust stance against racism in America cannot but influence white racists outside America. By the same token, continued racism in that country would send encouraging signals to others in Europe and elsewhere that the evil and dangerous ideology and practices have the implicit support or connivance of the only super-power in the world.

In 1973 Dr. Henry Kissinger, then US Secretary of State went to apartheid, white-ruled South Africa and told the white minority racist government that the United States could no longer support it at the UN and other international gatherings because of its racist policies and programs. It soon became obvious to that that regime that its days were numbered. For without the implied or latent support of the leader of the West the five million white people in South Africa could not indefinitely continue their abhorrent policies and programs. It is true that the apartheid government had then the best air-force, army and security service in the whole of Africa. But short of deploying this awesome materiel against the local black, fifty million people, there was no realistic way the regime could continue for more than a few years. As the military option was not feasible, the realistic alternative was a face-saving, peaceful transfer of power. Admittedly, racism as enshrined in the national constitution in South Africa did not end till 1994, but after the Kissinger visit the writing was clearly on the wall, that the days of white minority, supremacist rule based on racism were numbered.

The other main reason why activities and programs against racism in America merit special attention is that the overwhelming and preponderant control and ownership of the most powerful and influential media and communications outlets, with vast global reach, have been in American hands. Thus these powerful internet, radio, television, movies, if even mildly deployed in the fight against racism, can go a very long way in reducing racism in America itself and also in Europe, Australia and New Zealand.

85

Finally the stiff fines and damages handed by US courts against those found guilty of racist behavior or utterances, at least in public, do go viral and the news spreads all the world over. For after such fines or damages are inflicted, similar acts outside the United States of America, when leniently treated tend naturally to make a mockery of the judicial system of the country concerned. Furthermore, such a stance has the unintended consequence of giving the impression to all opponents of racism that the judicial system by ignoring racism actually condones it, or at best is not serious about contributing to the demise of racism, an ideology and practice condemned by all national constitutions across the world and against the UN Charter, to which all nations in the international community are signatories (although the Muslim nations have refused to acknowledge its legitimacy where they perceive a conflict with Sharia Law).

It is only right and proper that anti–racist activities in the United States are given as much moral boosting and support as possible by victims of racism. Also such a stance would encourage their fellow white compatriots to join them in fighting racism. No rational being would deny the heroic actions and sacrifices of the thousands of African-American leaders who from the dark days of slavery through the epic marches organized by Dr. Martin Luther King, to the present day mass protests and demonstrations. All these noble and brave actions deserve the great admiration and respect of all human beings who believe in democracy and human rights.

For their sacrifices and actions created the political and social environment that galvanized Congresses, almost all white and presidents who were all white, to bring in laws that chipped away at racism, little by little, step by step. With the overwhelming majority of the American electorate being of European extraction or origin, and in a political climate where racism has thrived well since the days of slavery in the fifteenth century, white politicians and presidents naturally needed a strong, compelling case to advance the cause of anti -racism. The point I am trying to make is that whilst it is perfectly rational for black people to be opposed to racism as victims of the abhorrent system, it is a different kettle of fish when powerful leaders, aware that their political power derives from the white majority are being persuaded to enact laws that many of their followers perceive are not in their best interest. Not easy, at all! Hence, my utmost admiration for the white leaders who, moral considerations apart, take a holistic and long term stand on racism. By their words and actions they have all made enduring contributions to ridding the USA of racism. For in America as in all other countries citizens tend to follow the example of their leaders.

CHAPTER 11

# THE VITAL ROLE OF
# THE VICTIMS

Whilst it is the right thing to do that we all join in the fight to uproot racism wholly and completely from the world and whilst the onus is indeed on the shoulders of the racists to change their ways, there is also an important role that the victims can play. Lying down and passively taking no action is not an option. Mass demonstrations and marches have their place in the struggle, but very important is the need for the victims, by their deeds and words, to demonstrate that racism is not only untenable, but ridiculous! For in a situation, where for centuries, non Europeans have been portrayed as stupid, lazy, unambitious, incompetent and irresponsible, with the males depicted as sexually-driven, wild and predatory, it simply does not serve the interests of the victims to say or do the very things that their detractors accuse them of. The centuries old- stereotyping of Africans and Asians is incorrect, bereft of any scientific basis and are merely subjective evaluations that are buttressed by self-serving academic, literary, political or economic power. For deprived of the oxygen of power, particularly political power, racism becomes meaningless and ineffectual.

Recent developments in South Africa since 1994 have amply demonstrated that racism, devoid of its political underpinning quickly begins to fade away, even if its economic and social underpinnings continue or stay in place. Nevertheless, victims of racism, irrespective of the statements above need to prove their enemies wrong through their own words and deeds. For example, if fellow citizens in the United Kingdom, meeting me, conclude that because of my skin colour, I am stupid or unintelligent (however warped and unwarranted their views are), then the onus is on me to prove them absolutely wrong. It simply does not help my cause to say or do the very things which they, out of ignorance or bigotry or fear, accuse me of. I would be strengthening their bigotry or prejudices by doing the very things that they say are typical of my race!

I am in no way suggesting that racists are justified in what they say or do. How can I? Not at all! But in a situation where the political and economic power are in practically all cases in the hands of white people, nonwhite people who corroborate the racists' accusations are in effect serving two masters, namely their own anti-racist stance and the racist stance of the racists. And as the Bible rightly states, 'No man can serve two masters.' All victims of racism, direct and indirect, need to prove the racists wrong on all counts by consistently showing that their abhorrent ideology is irrational.

That is the reason why non-Caucasians cannot afford to indulge in any activities or programs that undermine their progress and advancement. Thus antisocial activities such as smoking, inebriation, taking drugs, indiscipline, crime, violence, levelling unwarranted accusations of racism and irresponsible sexual activities, all need to be avoided like the bubonic plague. Whether white people participate in these activities or not is irrelevant to the argument. For as things stand now, and have been so for decades, victims of racism cannot afford to substantiate the cause of the racists by acting or talking as expected by the racists. As I see it, the onus is partly on the victim to assist the demolition of the baneful ideology, not to advance it.

Let's for a moment consider this true personal experience of mine. For the fifty eight or so years that I have been associated with Great Britain, including living here for thirty five years, my wife and I have lived in various parts of London. At one time in the mid 1960's we lived in an exclusive neighborhood where black people were hardly in sight As such, although at that time I was no longer an ambassador, I decided to appoint myself an unofficial ambassador of black people. My purpose was to show by words and deeds that the false ideas that had been planted in their minds that nonwhite people were somehow dirty, stupid and lazy were not true, but that it was a load of disinformation meant to facilitate racist ideas of white so-called supremacy.

As such, aware of the fact that for many of the English neighbours I was the only black person that they had contact with or had seen at close range, I was determined to help them unload the heavy burden of racism by showing by my own life and speech that those who had indoctrinated them against nonwhite people had done them immense harm. So with the full support of my dear wife we kept a decent home, clean and well furnished, with a white, uniformed nanny/house keeper to debunk some of the racist ideas and views that I am sure many held. For I knew that if any of the neighbours out of curiosity came into our three bedroomed, detached home and saw even a single fly, the story would soon fly around the whole area that 'the black man's house was teeming with flies!' We saw to it that our garden was well kept and maintained by a neighbor, who happened to be a trained gardener. Our car had the deserved maintenance and polish. Even our dog, 'Excellency' was well groomed, always wearing with pride his ambassadorial collar and properly trained by my wife, Breid to greet visitors warmly!

I agree that what we did was primarily for our own benefit. True! But it also served the secondary purpose of making intelligent white people who got to know us review or reassess their pre-conceptions or views about nonwhite people. And I like to think several years later that in my own small way I contributed in assisting them to do away with any racist pretensions or attitudes that that they possibly had acquired from their parents, schools, the media or places of work. Certainly by living and interacting with them the way that I did, I provided them with no corroborative support for the validity of racism. And for the past few decades whether in Europe or America, I have maintained the stance that as a member of a group that has been a victim of racism, I have a moral duty, by my words and deeds, to help prove the racists wrong and not rather solidify or enhance their dangerous views.

In recent years the stupendous economic and other achievements of the Japanese have laid to rest all the unjustified and derogatory remarks and comments about them. Emerging from the second world war utterly devastated, they took advantage of American assistance (also provided to post-war West Germany under the Marshall Plan) and American insistence that they adopt democracy as a form of government, by hard work, sacrifice, pursuit of the vital core enterprises,(namely, Science, Technology, Engineering, and Mathematics), through education, plus a willingness and readiness to learn from others, by the mid- 1970s Japan, had become the second largest economy in the world! A position that it held till 2010 when it was overtaken by China with a population of 1.3 billion, ten times that of Japan. Even more remarkable is the fact that Japan has very limited land and very limited natural and mineral resources compared with many countries in Europe and the Americas. This achievement demonstrates, once and for all, that however unjustifiably marginalized or vilified a people may be by their detractors and enemies, the victims can turn the tables on those who had considered them inferior. The phenomenal advancement of Japan was primarily generated by empowerment through the acquisition of education.

Another non-Caucasian state whose record of impressive progress and achievements in recent year belies the long peddled ideology and practice of racism is Singapore. This is a small city state of only 0.6000 square km and a population of just 4.8 million Yet, after its independence in 1965, despite the paucity of natural and mineral resources, Singapore has within a few decades from 1948 to the present, chalked up a Gross Domestic Product per head of $58,000.00 higher than that of most countries in Europe and even America. This remarkable and historic record came about through hard work, national mobilization for a restructuring of society by promoting education, discipline, sacrifice and good national leadership.

To some extent some force had to be utilized by the Government of Singapore to make people, even when they were unwilling, to do the right thing for the environment, for their families, and for the nation, as represented by the government of the day. For example, strict public health laws were put in place and robustly implemented, with stiff fines or even imprisonment for those who willingly broke them. Thus spitting in public was a criminal offence, although some academics and libertarians in the West may consider this an infringement on the human rights of the citizen. But by this program of intensive environmental responsibility the incidence of infectious diseases went down, the people got healthier and the overall national economic productivity grew. Certainly, the national growth in GDP per head would not have been the same if many of the working population were frequently ill or away from work as a result of clearly preventable illnesses or working below par. Unfortunately, these are the scenarios of neglect far too frequent in many countries in Africa, Asia and the Caribbean Islands!

As such certainly in the developing countries which are all populated by nonCaucasians, and which are the victims of racism by Caucasians, there is a strong and compelling case for the application by the state of what I call, 'Benign, Modulated Force'. In the interests of the whole society and the country, particularly for the benefit of the children and the future generations the state, through its agents are justified in using a measure of force to ensure that their own lives, those of their neighbours and the environment are safe-guarded. The history of Europe and America has shown that initially there is always some resistance to laws which although good for society are not welcome or appreciated by some citizens. But when the laws are robustly and fairly implemented the beneficiaries are the whole of society, including the very people who were opposed to them. Indeed, whilst often the economic and industrial transformation of Singapore under Lee Kuan Yew received fulsome and positive praise and commendation from many people outside Singapore it is often forgotten that some of the strategies and programmes that were used to bring about the success story in Singapore would be considered undemocratic and to some extent infringements on human rights.

For example in all countries there are strict laws against pollution and degradation of the environment by the performance in public of certain, perfectly normal biological functions. In the advanced countries the punishments for breaches are severe, including stiff fines or imprisonment. That the culprit may defend himself by protesting that he was doing simply what was natural and indeed vital for life and health would not sway any court of law or even his neighbours. If developed countries still find it necessary to apply a measure of force to facilitate the common or national good, then what about the developing countries which are grossly lacking in some basic public health infrastructure? Of course, the assumption here depends on the leaders genuinely caring about the life, welfare and progress of those that they are privileged to lead, which is not always the case.

The fact that China, with a population of almost 1.4 billion, is a communist nation and has been so since 1949 has led many white people to criticize some of the methods and programs that were used to bring about the phenomenal economic and industrial changes in that country. Although the horrendous deaths of at least forty million people during the Great Leap Forward and throughout earlier and later phases in China's Communist history are most heart – wrenching, they do not negate its present achievement, ever since a less draconian, less doctrinaire and more practical approach has been implemented. The application of force was deemed necessary by the government to manage the gargantuan, industrial, social and health problems of a nation, especially a country whose population accounts for 18.6% of the whole world.

The problem is when the application of force becomes violent, capricious, unbridled and partial, favoring one section or group, as it most certainly did in China, though less so today. However if a degree of modulated benign force is not to be applied in the developing countries to bring about a drastic improvement in the quality of life of the population as a whole then when will there be any significant progress and development? Meanwhile millions of babies die in infancy, pregnant women die unnecessarily, economic and industrial development is stymied and people continue to eke out a miserable and sad existence, as other fellow human beings live a good quality of life.

Perhaps India, with a population of 1.26 billion, illustrates the more 'democratic path' towards development. It has yet to catch up with China, but has made great strides since it began to aggressively promote business investment, especially in the technological communications sector which is currently driving the global economy and in which it is now a world leader.

However, even in the most advanced and democratic countries in the West, the State applies some element of force to ensure that people do the right thing. For example, in the UK, USA and other developed countries it is obligatory for parents to send their children to elementary or primary and secondary school, which in any case is free. There are free school meals, if needed and other incentives aimed to help children acquire basic education. Any parents who refuse to send their children to school, are warned by the appointed agents of the state (social workers) to do so. And if the parents stubbornly refuse consistently to abide by the law, force is applied to take the children from the parents into the care of the state and subject the parents to the due process of the law by having them prosecuted and, if found guilty, sent to prison or fined.

Screaming and scratching all the way to prison that the state has no right to take their children from them and that their human rights are being violated, holds no water. The march to prison continues and if whilst in prison they do not abide by the rules and regulations of their new correctional residence, the law is used to increase their period of stay! So, if even in the developed or advanced countries benign, modulated force continues to be applied by the state to keep society cohesive, peaceful, democratic and prospering, then why should similar force not be applied in the developing countries which are all nonwhite and victims of racism? For any person, who either from personal experience or from watching television news, documentaries or in movies, sees the appalling, degrading and inhuman conditions of some nonwhite people in parts of the developing world and states, with a wry smile, that those unfortunate people should be allowed the freedom to continue living in conditions reminiscent of the Middle Ages, is truly deplorable, showing an absence of humanity.

In fact, I venture to state that such a stance by white people smacks of latent racism, clothed in the hypocritcal words of condescension. I am of the considered view that governments are fully entitled and indeed have a moral obligation to utilize a degree of compulsion to advance the wellbeing and welfare of their peoples! This is especially so, as invariably the leaders themselves, as a result of education and better opportunities in life, are enjoying a modern, comfortable life whilst many of their fellow citizens wallow in filth, unhygienic conditions and ignorance, staring poverty and deprivation in the face most of their lives. I submit that if the leaders, elected or unelected, wish to claim legitimacy as leaders, then they indeed have a national and political duty to help raise their compatriots to levels of life befitting human beings in the twenty-first century.

Governments in the developed countries have been doing so for centuries, particularly from the nineteenth century. That is how inter alia, those countries (all white apart from Japan)have come to be where they are now and restrictions still apply that limit where people can or cannot build, even on their own lands. There are even limitations on where and when a person can play his radio or sing or dance or eat. In some societies in Great Britain, these behavioural restraints and restrictions are in some instances so ingrained and refined that the way and manner a person handles cutlery at the restaurant or dinner table can make all the difference between a job promotion or getting another invitation! White people have progressed by sticking to the relevant societal and legal rules and requirements. Naturally some human beings by the very nature of our fallible condition or from a deprived background, stray from the straight and narrow path. But they are generally a small minority.

If governments exclude moderated force from their arsenal for fighting preventable infectious diseases, child slavery, or stopping the pollution and degradation of the environment, or the sexual abuse of children, gender or racial discrimination, then they are in effect abnegating their duties as governments. For with the high salaries, allowances, privileges and honour of public office must go the responsibility of leadership. They, as leaders have seen the light, metaphorically speaking and therefore must not, repeat not, allow their followers to wallow in filth, ignorance, squalor and human indignity, even if the latter out of ignorance, choose to do so.

Let us consider this scenario, all too familiar in many parts of Africa and Asia. An agent of the Government, a health or social worker interacts with a poor family consisting of an unemployed man, a wife and seven children. They are living in very terrible, unhygienic conditions and the children have colourful talismans around their necks and bodies to ward off evil spirits and diseases. The children look emaciated, depressed and show hopelessness in their sad eyes. What should the agent of the government do? Either leave them alone to wallow in their sad deplorable condition and continue to die unnecessarily, or using the powers vested in him/her to coax, cajole and persuade the parents to strip away the talismans, burn them, sweep their compounds and burn the rubbish and begin to give the best food, not to the Big Man or husband, as the head of the household, but to the children?

I submit that if all the soft options mentioned above to ameliorate the conditions of the children and indeed those of the parents fail to produce positive results, then the application of Benign, Modulated Force is not only justified but vitally and urgently necessary in the interests of humanity and mankind. For after all, those mired in filth, ignorance and abject poverty are also human beings, like their educated and comfortable compatriots or those thousands of miles away from them living by comparison, extremely privileged lives.

So whilst vigorously condemning racism by white people, the victims also have a major role to play to bring the abominable ideology and practice to a quick demise, by raising the dignity, education and well-being of nonwhites. It would mean governments forcing children to be sent to school by their parents, forcing people to clean their homes whether they are only modest huts or not, forcing them not to smoke or drink in excess, forcing them communally to dig wells, cut the grass and weeds in the environment, stop washing themselves in the very rivers that they drink from, stop having children they cannot afford to look after, eradicate indiscipline, as evidenced by lateness, laziness, bribery, and corruption. A robust program like this inter alia would in a matter of fifty years catapult most countries that are victims of racism into at least middle income nations, whose confident peoples would no longer worry about racism. For by their progress and advancement they would have removed the rationale for racism. Of course, such achievements, outstanding by any standards may not be sufficient to convince the diehard white racist who somehow thinks or believes firmly that, notwithstanding evidence to the contrary, he is 'better' or 'superior' to the non-Caucasian, with better education, a better standard of living and a higher quality of life! But that person would become an object of ridicule among his own people, a dinosaur, out of place and out of time.

May I end this piece on the need sometimes for the application of benign, modulated force on people for their own good by briefly narrating a personal experience. Till I went to Achimota College in Accra, Ghana in 1945 I only knew, like all my peers, the genre of music called High Life. It was then very popular, and still is. It is smooth, rhythmic music that cannot fail to encourage movement and dancing. At Achimota (a large, prestigious, coeducational boarding institution established in Ghana by the British in 1925, for the whole of colonial Africa) we were instructed every Sunday afternoon to spend an hour at the Music School, listening to what we were told was called Classical Music. We listened to it and were taught piano playing. All of us coming from the countryside hated this hour-long ordeal of music which jarred on the ears and meant nothing to us. It was not the type of 'move and shake' music that we were used to. After a number of months we got used to this new musical language and began to like it very much, although at first some of us tried to abscond from the compulsory lessons, even at the risk of half an hour digging for our inexplicable absence.

As I grew into adulthood, classical music has been one of the few passions in my life and I am eternally grateful to our house masters and music masters, both black and white, who forced me, yes, applied benign, modulated force, to inculcate in me the love of this music. It was several years later that I learnt in the media that research in the United States of America had conclusively established that exposing babies to this type of music, specifically Mozart's, when in-vitro has considerable positive impact on their mental development. Sadly, I got my exposure, initially strongly resisted by me, when I was twelve years old. Looking back I wish it had been twelve years earlier. I am sure it would have made me more intelligent and successful or let's say, more adventurous! Sometimes, looking back, I have felt that if my housemasters and music teachers had not forced me to imbibe the love for classic music, they would have rightly been open to accusations of gross neglect or dereliction of intellectual duty towards me and my young fellow students!

Another incident in Ghana, a potentially rich country, which impressed on me the urgent and justified need sometimes for the state, as represented by its appointed agents, to use benign, modulated force to ensure the welfare and safety of its people came in July 1960. I was invited to a meeting at the Information (Public Relations) Department of the Government. The head of the department was a kind, jovial, ex-Cambridge Englishman, whom I had never met. Apparently he had taken notice of my articles in the Ghanaian papers and a couple or so prestigious journals in the United Kingdom. My first book THE NEW GHANA, which became an international bestseller, had earlier been published in March 1958, on Ghana's first anniversary as an independent country.

After a brief interview, Jimmy Moxon offered me a book contract. The lavish book contract involved touring the country in a long, smart American chauffeur-driven car interviewing people and collecting material for a book on Ghana's evolution from a British colony into a republic within the Commonwealth. Visiting the north of the country for the first time, I was driving through a remote area when I saw three, tall completely naked women. I was naturally shocked and could not believe my eyes. I asked my driver to stop. Fortunately for me, there was a young girl of about sixteen who was clothed and spoke English. She said that she was on her way to collect water from a nearby well. Through her I asked the women why they were walking about naked. They smiled and said that they had been doing so all their lives. I asked them whether they found anything wrong with their state. They were surprised at my question and rather amused. When I asked them to allow me to photograph them they responded that I must pay them money as the white people always did. My plea to be exempted from the fee as I was a fellow citizen was to no avail. So I paid the fee and took the photos, which I kept for a number of years. To me they were not pornographic or in any way titillating. They were to me rather a constant reminder of the work that needed to be done to stop human beings going about in a way and manner not befitting human beings. The photos gave me much sadness and were in no way funny or amusing. Interestingly, my young interpreter told me that since she started putting on clothes her mother, aunts and grandmother had been pressurizing her to do without them. But she had refused to do so, as she told me, 'because it is not right for people to walk about naked.'

A few months after my visit the Ghanaian Government led by Dr. Kwame Nkrumah, launched a robust campaign in the area to get the women to put on clothes. Students, social workers and police all took part in the campaign. Clothes of various colours, shapes and sizes, were brought in, donated by charities in America and the United Kingdom. So in a matter of a few months a seemingly intractable social problem that had existed for centuries, and had received 'benign neglect' from the white British, district commissioners (agents of the colonial governor in the capital, Accra) was completely eradicated, with broad smiles on the faces of the women.

For Dr. Kwame Nkrumah, the founding father of Ghana, firmly believed that it was degrading and inhuman for fellow citizens to go about naked. Furthermore, the continued existence of the challenge only served to fuel the bigotry and prejudices of racists, who enjoyed the situation to justify their stance. For none of them were so approving on ideological grounds that they divested themselves of clothes! Rather, it was an opportunity for them to feel superior. Since the eradication of this age old practice, the people in that isolated area have been avidly clamouring for more and more education. Their voracious appetite for education, clean water and health facilities has reached such a crescendo that local members of Parliament(Congress) who during election campaigns have volubly promised these vital essentials for a good quality of life, but have been unable to deliver on their promises have been ejected from office. In fact, in a few cases these slick but luckless elected leaders have been booed on public platforms when they sought to garner the support and votes of the people. Such has been the dramatic effect of the application of 'benign, modulated force' by the Nkrumah regime in tackling an age-old social problem that had provided much mirth and amusement to many white tourists for many decades. Rather distressing was the fact that the district commissioners in Ghana (and in the other colonies of the European Powers) all white, and appointed and paid to look after the welfare and progress of the people in their district, allowed this nakedness to flourish, despite knowing that it degraded the women's humanity, insulted their womanhood and was an inappropriate maternal role model to their daughters. To state that their inaction was due to reluctance and intractable stubbornness on the part of the women is no excuse or justification. These were highly trained university graduates from some of the best universities in Europe, but they did nothing. They allowed the women to wallow in their ignorance/innocence, victims of the onslaughts of vicious flies during the day and helpless prey to the multi-pronged relentless mosquito attacks at night. Were the white appointed agents of the colonial governments pandering to their own racism or were they knowingly or unconsciously participating in a programme undermining any progress and advancement of the people under their care?

*This situation has been made much worse by the popular doctrines of moral relativism and cultural equivalence. Under these obnoxious ideologies, both white and nonwhite people have been encouraged to believe, not that all people are equal (which is the basis of my argument)* *but that all cultures are equal in virtue and value. This is patently not the case. No rational person would seriously claim that ancient Stone Age cultures were just as benign, sophisticated and desirable as societies based on democracy, universal education and human rights. It is not that Stone Age people were less intelligent. Far from it! But their historical circumstances were different. In other words, there is a sense in which democracy, the obligation to treat all the same under the law, freedom and the opportunity to determine one's own path in life are <u>absolutely better</u> than a society in which these qualities are absent. Yet this is the very opinion the moral relativists deny. They do irreparable harm to nonwhite people in undermining their desire to improve their situation, by encouraging them to demand respect for cultural attitudes which prevent their own progress and fly in the face of evidence.*

The same goes for those who condescendingly insist in judging nonwhite people by a different standard from what they apply to themselves. This is a new form of racism under the disguise of political correctness. A recent and terrible example is the cover-up of the sexual abuse of a large number of white English girls by the authorities 1) because they did not wish to be accused of racism as all the perpetrators were from the Asian continent, and 2) even under certain British judges there has been an unmistakable tendency to hand out lenient sentences to nonwhite violators of women because, in Islamic culture, those certain behaviours are accepted, if not actively condoned.

So I can assure readers, especially white people who see on television or read in the papers terrible conditions of utter deprivation, hunger and diseases of millions of people in the developing world that their plight is in no way in-born or genetic but entirely due to IGNORANCE AND LACK OF OPPORTUNITIES AND A DEGREE OF DISINTEREST BY SOME OF THEIR OWN ELECTED OR APPOINTED LEADERS. If they are forced to tame and improve dramatically their environment, and absorb education, with their whole bodies, souls and minds, I am absolutely convinced that most of them would prove as capable and successful as white people or their own compatriots who have by hard work, education and perhaps a bit of luck, escaped the appalling plight and conditions that they lived in.

Given that victims of racism have an important role to bring about its quick end by their own words and deeds, it means that nonwhite people who do the very things that some white people accuse them of, are simply not helping the cause of defeating racism. Thus although racists may also indulge in irresponsible fatherhood, spousal abuse, exploitation of child labor or women, and other anti-social activities, if victims of racism also participate to their hearts content in these activities then they are compounding the problem of racism. For to the extent that for the past five centuries economic and political power has been in the hands of white people, that is peoples of European extraction, and therefore it is they who have set the agenda and criteria in social, legal, economic and political norms, the onus is on the victims of racism to show by their words and especially actions, that their detractors and tormentors are wrong.

Equally it is incumbent upon the victims of racism not to be seduced by the protestations of the 'all cultures are equal' crowd, who will only encourage their continuing victimhood by provoking them to wear it as a badge of courage, instead of throwing it in the trash can and standing on their dignity as individual human beings, not as cultural group symbols! Often in these cases, the victims of racism are being used as tools by those who have a grudge against society for a number of reasons, and wish to overthrow it.

Ending all these manifestations of racism can be done at the national levels and also at the individual level. That is why it is so important that educated Africans and Asians, plus those in the Pacific region and in the diaspora, aspire to achieve as high as possible, when they get the chance in all fields of human endeavor, particularly in the vital core fields of Science, Technology, Engineering and Mathematics(STEM). Recent impressive records chalked up in these fields, especially in Asia have indeed set a major intellectual dilemma for white racists who still cannot unburden themselves of the heavy load of racism. For as the lawyers say, 'Res ipso loquitor '(The facts speak for themselves). It is therefore, understandable why there have been numerous instances of the suppression or attempts to suppress the outstanding achievements of Africans and Asians in recent years. For the racists are fully aware that such noble records, with no racial bias in their evaluation, drive bulldozers through their ideology, making them appear rather foolish.

However, the fast and ever-growing development of the internet, global television, radio and the social media are making it more and more difficult to marginalize or cover up the positive achievements of victims of racism. For the more such achievements are known, the more difficult and unrealistic it would be for racists to continue repeating that, 'Well, to every rule there is an exception' or 'One swallow does not make a summer' or 'Yes, but they have European blood in their veins', when referring to great achievers of biracial origins, or that 'They copied from the white man' or ..........

Another major incident in recent memory that goes to highlight the work that needs to be done by victims of racism to help debunk and degrade the ideology may be narrated here. Before the time the Nazis came into power in Germany in 1933 their leaders, supported by highly educated academics, intellectuals and writers had been propagating the racist ideology that white people were superior to nonwhites, thus justifying the latter's subjugation. Furthermore the theory went on to state that even among the white people the blonde, blue-eyed, so-called Aryans were superior to the rest. By this theory and practice black people were at the rock bottom in the racial hierarchy in intelligence, competence, abilities and morality.

Then came the Olympic Games in 1936 in Berlin. At a time when there was no television the world radio and press at the Games constituted the ideal medium to convey to the whole world the rightness of their newfangled racist programme. The Nazi leaders having spent vast sums to train their teams and stage the world event were hoping and expecting the successes and achievements of German sportsmen would confirm and corroborate their strongly held views, before huge admiring crowds. They were looking forward to sensational successes for the world at large to witness. Bitterly disappointing for them, the successes were not the type that they were anticipating.

Despite the rabid racism in America at the time the American teams to the Games included many outstanding black men and women. Among them was Jesse Owens, a fit–looking remarkable African-American, who in a number of races before the very eyes of the whole world, was seen way ahead of the white runners, including Germans! Any person who has been fortunate to watch the documentary on the event would be amazed at how the Nazi leaders, especially the Fuhrer, Adolf Hitler, could simply not contain their anger, fury, exasperation and disappointment as Jesse Owens made a laughing stock of the Nazis and their intellectual under-writers. The message that was conveyed for all and sundry by the multiple gold medalist Jesse Owens was clear for all to see and hear. At the ceremony of handing the honors to the winners, it was customary for the head of state in doing so to shake the hands of the winners. The German leader shook the hands of all the winners except one, Jesse Owens. He flatly refused to do so.

Come to think of it, why should he shake the hand of the man who had for a few minutes torpedoed Hitler's racist theories and ideology and thus made a mockery of him before his own people and the outside world? So although some published accounts of the life of the German dictator suggest that in private he was good to many of the people around him, on this historic occasion he showed his true colours as a racist of the very worst type. It is a pity the world did not draw the appropriate conclusions from this demonstration of Hitler's inhumanity. *From the Olympic rostrum to the gates of hell in Auschwitz and other places of bureaucratized genocide was just a few small steps.*

The unchallengeable records of Jesse Owens and others, followed by tremendous successes in boxing by Joe Louis and by others in various fields, led to the general consensus among many white people that black people were all 'brawn and no brains'. In other words, they were good at physical activities like running, boxing, athletics and sexual prowess, but not at any cerebral activities, like science, technology, engineering, literature, medicine and mathematics. Little note was taken by the detractors of nonwhite people of the fact that in America as a result of slavery and then racism, black people had been denied opportunities in education, health and employment, liberally accorded their fellow white citizens. Nor did racists take into account the fact that in Asia, Africa and the Pacific Regions, colonialism had kept the people for decades with limited chances in life. Thus ironically, the great achievements of nonwhite people in the fields of sports, physical endurance and music went rather to support the racism.

Although the fallacy that black people are more brawn than brains, still persists among many white people it is rapidly disappearing in the face of evidence to the contrary. Not only because modern communication, movements, education and globalization are depleting the numbers of white racists, but also because political power has dramatically shifted in the countries that were formerly colonies of white people. Propelling this global change has also been the increasingly obvious and undeniable achievements in all fields of human endeavour by nonwhite people. In science, technology, engineering, mathematics, literature and medicine peoples for centuries marginalized and ridiculed by white people are demonstrating that if the playing field is level, nonwhite people can do as well as their opponents and in many cases even better.

Thus it is this fervent desire by the victims of racism to prove that they are as good as their detractors which partly accounts for the ambition of nations like China and India to spend huge sums of money and other national resources to develop nuclear weapons or put men into space. Of course the primary motivation is national security and protection. But the cause of national pride cannot be ruled out. This is evidenced for example, by this historic event recounted here : When in 1998, the Republic of India exploded its first nuclear bomb, it is interesting and noteworthy that the head of the nuclear programme kept emphasizing at a press conference that their achievement was all home grown, without any external help or assistance. Without mentioning any nation or continent it was still apparent that Dr. Abdul Kalam was referring or had in mind peoples who had developed nuclear devices and for centuries had held in doubt the intelligence and capabilities of India and other nonwhite peoples.

Emphasis was placed on the fact that their achievement had cost far less and taken far less time than their white counterparts had taken. In effect what the eminent Indian nuclear scientist implied was :'Look at what we have done ! We, who have been maligned for centuries as being stupid, incapable and unintelligent have been able, despite centuries of unsurmountable challenges, abuse and exploitation, to do at very little cost and with far less resources than what the white man took many years to accomplish.' The wave of national euphoria that followed the announcement of the success of India reverberated not only in the country itself but far beyond its borders. The same uproarious excitement was in evidence in India and China when both of them separately put a man in space a few years later. For these epochal achievements enhanced not only national pride but dealt serious blows to the whole theory and practice of racism.

Collectively, peoples in Asia, Africa, parts of South America and the Pacific region constitute about eighty-five percent of the global population of seven billion. Even if the evaluation is based on the number of countries that are populated predominantly by Europeans or people of European origin or extraction, or on the number of countries where power is in the hands of Europeans, the figure jumps to twenty five percent. This is due to the fact that Europe although relatively small in area is divided into many countries.

As such, even if the racists do not at all like it, the areas where they can talk or act with impunity have since the middle of the twentieth century shrunk dramatically. It is becoming increasingly unwise for a white racist to go to any area outside Europe and talk or act in a way considered racist, unless of course he wants to experience life in an African or Asian or Middle Eastern prison. And as one who has unfortunately endured life in an African prison for fifteen months, even as a political prisoner I certainly would not at all recommend it to the faint-hearted. For the mouthwatering meals, gymnastics facilities, good medical care, sports, colour television, libraries etc do not exist! To endure months of hardship in an environment where heartless flies mount coordinated onslaughts in the day and are replaced by fat, vicious mosquitoes at night, determined to suck your blood is no laughing matter. The sports medical and educational facilities that prisoners may take for granted in the developed countries simply do not generally exist in the developing countries. This is not because the governments or people in these countries are not interested in prison reforms but chiefly due to the fact that with millions of people outside the prisons living on two dollars or less a day, the said governments have other more urgent priorities on their national agendas.

The view that rapid economic and industrial development and advancement do not necessarily require enormous natural and mineral resources is supported by the fact that indeed Japan has limited natural and mineral resources. Increasingly, the evidence is mounting and becoming more compelling that the greatest factor and most important factor in economic and industrial development of nations is the human resource. Otherwise, it is difficult to explain rationally why the GDP per head of a small country such as Ireland, with a population of only 4.7 million and no significant natural or mineral resources, has a GDP per head of 40,460 dollars, whilst my country of birth, with a population of 25 million and huge resources in the form of arable land, equable climate, and rich deposits of gold, diamonds, bauxite, manganese, plus a flourishing vegetation of cocoa, fruits and vegetables and other resources has a GDP per head of only $1,700. However, as stated frequently in this work, the predicament of developing countries like Ghana and others all inhabited by non Europeans is not a question of skin colour but as Dr Jared Diamond makes abundantly clear, an issue of environmental factors. The racists are wrong when they attribute the under development of certain areas in the world to a racial factor. They are equally wrong when in their own countries, they explain the high rates of crime, irresponsible fatherhood, poverty, and hopelessness to skin colour. For such a stance ignores the environmental and other social factors as well as legal interventions which cumulatively have resulted in this predicament.

To take a position of correlating development in different areas of the world, to factors apart from race not only is right, but it gives hope to the billions of people (85% of the world's polpulation) who are not European or of European extraction. Although this work is primarily concerned with racism, as viewed from the non-white perspective, I will be failing in my moral duty if I do not make mention of a variant of racism which has done enormous and catastrophic damage and harm to humanity. For the second world war, (1939 – 1945)has its genesis in the anti-Semitism which prevailed in Germany at the beginning of the 1930's and was fueled fanned and exploited by the Nazis. Why 6 million Jews should be murdered simply for being Jews is one of the most heinous crimes against humanity ever recorded. The Holocaust, should be a constant reminder to humanity that racism is one of the most gargantuan and destructive and apocaplytic forces in the history of the world. Therefore, it is incumbent, on all human beings learning from history to do everything humanly possible to eradicate racism.

This book is based mostly on my life experiences and from talking with numerous men and women who have been victims of racism or have been strong and active in the campaigns against racism. They include numerous men and women that I have talked with in the United States of America, Eastern and Western Europe, India, Saudi Arabia and Africa. Additionally, over the course of 60 years I have read numerous books, articles and journals appertaining to the issue of global racism. In every country where there is a physically visible minority, they suffer a form of racism from the majority population. However, starting from about the 15th century it has been non Europeans or people of non-European extraction who have been the victims of racism but it is hoped that racism in whatever shape or form will have been eliminated from the earth by the next three decades.

For, according to the population experts by 2050 the nonwhite population in the United States of America will for the first time be more than the people of Caucasian origin. As president Barack Obama, points out in his celebrated book: **The Audacity of Hope**. This demographic change is bound to have profound legal, social, political, economic and other effects in America and subsequently the rest of the world. If the past is any guide, then the aforementioned changes will quicken the demise of racism.

# CHAPTER 12

# CONCLUSION

Racism as a global phenomenon, should concern all of us, both the perpetrators and the victims. For it is an ideology which if not dealt with robustly and effectively can lead to the murders of millions of people and the destruction of countless lives and properties. It is in fact, the highway to genocide. In this work I have tried to review the theory and practice of racism over the past five centuries, for in my humble view it is not a new phenomenon. Racism as a politically based phenomenon in which nonwhite people were and are the victims began shortly after the Trans-Atlantic Slave Trade in the fifteenth century, following the development of sugar-cane, cotton and tobacco plantations in the southern states of America, South America and the Caribbean Islands. And it intensified dramatically after the industrial revolution that began in the nineteenth century in Europe, beginning in the United Kingdom.

The outstanding inventions and discoveries of the period from the nineteenth century such as the steam engine, fueled the view that nonwhite people are inferior to white people. This was a superficial assessment of people whose exploitation and subjugation was thus rationalized. But as Professor Jared Diamond clearly establishes in his outstanding book GUNS, GERMS AND STEEL, all peoples were at about the same level of development up to the fifteenth century and that the subsequent different rates of development and advancement are accounted for by environmental differences. This view, the result of decades of unbiased study and scholarship among Europeans and people of non-European origin or extraction is supported not only by facts and data but also by commonsense. For if all human beings originated thousands of years ago in the plains of East Africa, the borders of Kenya and Ethiopia, with identical genetic makeups to begin with, then the differences in achievements among the progeny of the human beings over the millennia cannot be explained on race basis, as the racists love to expound but rather on factors which exclude the genetic component.

As such a view does not fit in comfortably with ideas of white supremacy many white academics, intellectuals and writers toed the conventional line and unashamedly espoused racism. A few decades ago, around 1962, an African student who was studying medicine in West Berlin came across a big tome on medicine which bore the name of an established and highly respected professor. In the book the eminent academic had produced data, research results and arguments that according to him established without any shadow of doubt the superiority of the so-called Aryan race, above any other race. The shocked African student, finding it very difficult to continue reading the book stopped. At the earliest opportunity he politely asked his professor how and why such manifestly unscientific views were expressed and published as scientific orthodoxy. The professor was silent for a few moments, then slowly said, 'John, at the time that was the prevailing view and we all had to go by it, unless you wanted to lose your job and possibly end up in a concentration camp....'. He was very uncomfortable with both the question and the answer. I submit that this story is not unique but must have been replicated in diverse forms in many parts of post-war Europe.

It stands to reason that many if not most of white racists who espouse racism, especially the better educated among them, know that they are wrong and have no unbiased, impartial scientific basis for their claims. However, to the extent that it is expedient and profitable to do so, (or under Hitler, dangerous not to do so) they would continue to propagate their views. Particularly so if the power structures in their country at the time give open support and unbridled encouragement and the oxygen of mass publicity to those views and 'facts' and approve their airing in public. The correlation between racism and political/economic power is illustrated inter alia by recent events in the Republic of South Africa. Since the collapse of apartheid in that country in 1994, suddenly the public statements, books, newspaper articles and academic treatises and even religious pronouncements that before the historic year were very common in South Africa have suddenly disappeared. Why?

Of course in a population of five million people of European extraction, statistically there are a few who still hanker after the good old days and are prepared to propagate their obnoxious views even at the risk of going to prison. But they are now a small, tiny minority, at least in public. This goes to show that benign modulated force (euphemistically called Law) can be very useful in making people stop doing what they know to be wrong but would do so, or continue to do so, if they thought that they could get away with it. Another true-life incident may be narrated here to show that racism without any political power underpinning is futile and unsustainable, at least for long. A few years ago, the British Broadcasting Corporation (BBC) highly respected all over the world for its impartiality, and commitment to facts, truth and fairness, broadcast an interesting television programme on its Channel Two. In it a white Afrikaner (white South African of Dutch ancestry) told the story of how she was vilified, humiliated and spat upon by her compatriots for marrying a black South African. She was swiftly expelled from her village, and went to live in a black village with her husband, according to her story.

Suddenly after the coming into power of the democratic, black majority rule led by the legendary Madiba Nelson Mandela, she said many of the very people who had only a couple or so years ago traduced and treated her with ignominious contempt, now wanted to befriend her and invited her back to her former village. The programme ends with the woman saying, that not only did she refuse to go back but that 'it was now my turn to spit on them '...Whilst naturally disapproving of the references to spitting, one cannot lose sight of the thrust and import of the story. Namely, the dramatic change in political power in the villages and the country as a whole. In other words, the same woman who had been previously treated as a social leper and a racial outcast had overnight become a very useful asset. Now she could be a useful conduit, if for no other reason, than getting in touch with the new power structure. So her former tormentors and enemies were now prepared and ready if not to stop their racism then at least firmly curb it for their own good!

Incidents as narrated above go to demonstrate that, firstly, white racists do know very well that what they are doing or saying is wrong, immoral and inhuman and secondly that they will only stop when they realise that for their own welfare and prosperity as human beings, advancing the cause of racism is not in their enlightened self-interest. Not in the long term anyway. For the past and current victims of racism, who happen to be in the developing countries, will not remain underdeveloped indefinitely. Sooner or later, more likely the former, they will also join the ranks of developed or at least middle-income countries. With this happening, part of the prop for racism would be removed.

So whilst the eradication of racism is squarely on the shoulders of Europeans and people of European extraction, as stated earlier, the victims must also play their part in bringing to an end the swift demise of the scourge which threatens peace and the progress of mankind. This leads to the question of whether there will be a race war, as some white racists speculate. Interestingly, the view of an impending or likely race war in the future is often voiced by rabid racists, who possibly expect to benefit from it. In my considered opinion, there will not be a race war. This is a view that I have come to after thirty five years living and working in Europe and the USA and after travelling to many countries in Africa, Western and Eastern Europe, India and Saudi Arabia. As a victim of racism myself, I have talked extensively with many other victims and also with people who have campaigned or talked against racism and those who, sitting on the fence, are not active racists but what I choose to call opportunistic racists. They are not pro or anti racism but can be forced to act or talk racially if the opportunity is ripe and the benefits out-weigh the risks. I have even had the chance to talk or reason with rabid white racists, who are firmly and unshakably of the view that history is on their side and that they are unquestionably doing the right thing, in fanning sentiments of racial superiority and a race war. These interactions plus careful reading of reports of statements by eminent world renowned scientists and books on racism have convinced me that racism is destined for the dust bin of social history and that a race war is absolutely not going to occur in the future.

It is simply inconceivable that all peoples of European origins would coalesce together to wage war on non-Caucasians, to register their racial superiority. Why?

Firstly as more countries under the aegis of the United Nations resort more to negotiation and dialogue, instead of physical violence to resolve disputes, however grave, global peace gains a firmer footing and the risk or prospect of war, racial or otherwise, diminishes into oblivion. As the famous British statesman, Winston Churchill said, after a resounding record as a war leader, 'Jaw-jaw is better than war- war'. The possibility of regional conflicts cannot be ruled out and are in fact taking place, but that is an entirely different scenario from a cataclysmic conflict that engulfs the majority of the nations and peoples of the world! After all since 1945, that is for over seventy years, the world has been able to avoid a global war. True, there have sadly been a few regional wars in Asia, Africa, the Middle East and Europe but thank God there has been no world war. And there is no reason, why with careful planning and strategies, that the world leaders cannot keep the status quo for another seventy years and further.

Secondly the development of weapons of mass destruction like the nuclear bomb, if any thing at all, have made war less and less an option of choice for settling even grave and intractable disputes among nations. The nightmare catastrophe unleashed on Japan by the dropping of the two atomic bombs on that country in AUGUST 1945, plus the long lasting consequences and reverberations occasioned by those two historic events make nuclear war rationally no more a viable instrument of human interaction. For two hundred thousand human beings to die in most horrific conditions in a matter of a few days is a scenario that no rational beings, black or white or whatever race, would want repeated, ever. And since 1945, more horrendous weapons of mass destruction have been invented. They are thousands of times more lethal than the first atomic bombs and have been mass produced by eight other countries. The nuclear scientists tell us that the nuclear or hydrogen bomb is thousands of times more powerful than the atomic bombs that were dropped on Japan in August 1945. This unnerving and disturbing fact of the destructive potential of nuclear weapons makes it unimaginable that they would ever be used to annihilate mankind.

Thirdly, from my own research and experience I have come to the inescapable conclusion that white women are not racists. Well not in any way as racists as males. Although personally I have experienced on five clear instances of racism and discrimination from white women these experiences are irrelevant pitted against the huge instances of good, fair and compassionate treatment from the hands of white women. Such unfortunate negative experiences do not in any way undermine the overwhelming evidence that the female human is not racist. With women forming about 52% of the white population and constituting the majority in all countries except a few countries globally (eg China and India) it means that as more and more women become empowered through education and economic and political growth, they are likely to be in control and command positions in most countries. Their unique role as a collective force for peace would destroy any trends or moves towards war.

Anthropologists, zoologists, primatologists and naturalists tell us that as human beings we are the highest developed among the primates. And that among the primates the monkeys, particularly the Bonono monkeys are 'our nearest cousins.' Their DNA,(94% that of human's) behaviour and family life come closest to those of human beings. Sadly, our nearest cousins did not develop to the stage of writing, reading and driving cars, flying aeroplanes or building houses! Watching their behavior in their natural state it is noticeable that when a male intruder or stranger is trying to enter the group or pack it is the male who challenges him and tries to drive him away from interfering with his 'wives and children'. In the ensuing fight the females stand aside as onlookers or shout and scream as if saying, 'Please, stop all this fighting. There is no need for it. We are all animals (Bonono monkeys) made by the same Creator. We must learn to coexist in harmony.' As not even the most eminent primatologist or naturalist can tell us what the females are really conveying in their screams, I like to think my speculation is not so irrational!.

In each and every case after the fight if the male –interloper or stranger is driven away, or killed the females continue with the head of family. But if he is beaten, driven out or killed, the females happily or unhappily welcome the new family head. Such basic protective instincts in the near-human Bonono monkey, hugely refined, polished and vastly developed and over thousands of years of mutations in human beings can thus account for why the white female is not racist, or far less so than the male. And gradually over the thousands of years, the strategies to repel the intruder or stranger, who looks obviously different from the rest have taken the forms of discriminatory laws or active measures to ensure that the females are kept away from the male intruder. If you find this irrational, then ask why we frequently hear the cry from white racists that 'they are taking our women and jobs'. Never 'They are taking our men' !

The natural instinct of the female to be 'maternal' or 'mothering'; or prone to care and nurture may explain why white women are not racists. For given a scenario where a woman has let's say five children and all except one become rich financiers or scientists or academics or lawyers it is very doubtful that the mother would less love the one child who was not as successful as the rest. It is therefore not at all surprising that the female is far less a racist than the male. As in every society children spend more time with their mothers than with their fathers it is rational to expect that over a period of several decades more and more children, from the influence of their mothers or their surrogate, adopted or foster mothers, would be less and less racist

In every country or nation women are far less crime prone than men. It may be noted that in every country laws exist that specify racism as a crime. So as racism is a crime in each and every country it follows that as women are less crime prone, they would feature less as racists. That different countries implement or apply anti-racism laws differently, does not detract from the fact that the laws exist against racism in every country.

Further evidence supporting the view that white women are not racists comes from reported cases in Europe and America of high-profile people who are alleged or accused of having made racist remarks or behaved thus in public. Consistently the culprits, whether renowned scientists, academics, politicians or writers are all male. Why? Indeed, as females are slightly more in number in Europe, the Americas, Australia and New Zealand, one would statistically expect more of them to be getting into trouble on race issues. Rather, to date, the facts and figures are the very opposite of what one would expect if white females are racist. The fact that occasionally here and there, evidence may be adduced of racist behavior or utterances by a few white women or girls, does not invalidate or nullify the overwhelming and preponderant global evidence that white women are not racist. Otherwise it becomes rather difficult to rationally explain why there are so many unions between black men and white women but relatively very few and rare unions between white men and black women.

The growing positive trends all over the world to remove discriminatory laws and practices against women, at home, the workplace or at leisure venues will also accelerate the elimination of racism. Up till a few years ago in as advanced and developed a nation as Great Britain, women suffered unjustifiable discrimination in pay and human rights. By the firm moral stand of outstanding women, supported by many principled men in public life, all such discriminatory practices and laws have disappeared, except for a few vestiges. From past experience of societal changes for the better, the great era when racism will be a thing of the past cannot come overnight. It will take some time.

To some extent the absence of racism in white women is perfectly understandable. Take for example a boat in distress with ten black men and ten white women. If say nine of the women are saved it is rational to expect the fortunate women to do everything within their power not only to save the lone woman in peril but also the ten men. Alas, for hundreds of years the boat has metaphorically been the world, non-Caucasians the black men on the boat.

But racial equality will happen and people looking back or reading about it, will be as ashamed about racism as we are now about the slave trade. Sometimes one reads in the media of the possibility of a race war. Invariably this is the opinion of some people who express unjustified fears of a world in which nonwhite people are on a rampage to hurt white people. This imaginary fear is used to justify a call to arms for pre-emptive war on nonwhite people before, from their point of view it is too late. Such fears are not at all realistic. For the possibility of such an unimaginable global genocide does not exist. No countries in Asia, Africa, the Americas or the Pacific Region or the Middle East can seriously and realistically be suspected of planning to wage a global war, let alone for 'race supremacy' reasons. For any future war would end disastrously for both the victor and the conquered. Yes, there would be a victory for one side after the unimaginably terrifying carnage and destruction of cataclysmic proportions but it would be 'a' Pyrrhic victory. And the hugely destructive repercussions and nuclear fallout would do irreparable damage to the planet and the whole of mankind, including the victors.

In the penultimate stages of apartheid in South Africa there was loose talk of the high probability of a race war if black majority rule materialized. Alarmist stories and blood culling scenarios of wild maurading black people on a rampage of murder of white people and destruction of their properties and assets were conjured and publicised. Then came the installation of a democratically elected African government in 1994, led by the legendary Madiba Nelson Mandela. Although the white population is five million and the nonwhite forty five million, and political and judicial power were now in the hands of the majority, none of the feared or rumored or anticipated (by white racists) mayhem, massacre or destruction took place. It is true that following the end of apartheid, many white South Africans left the country, for one reason or another. But many have also returned to the land of their birth, where they even may still have held property and farmland.

Whilst one may speculate on their reasons for returning, it is rational and fair to state that they must have done so on the conviction that it was better for them to live under a black majority democratic government than under a white majority government in a new land and environment. In any case, any such attempt by ultranationalist, racist indigenous, nonwhite Africans post apartheid, to mount a campaign of murder, rape and violence would have not only been genocide for which they would have been accountable under international law, but it would have been against all the precepts of the major religions of the world. Furthermore, such manifestly racist actions would have been counterproductive in many ways. A vicious cycle of violence and counter violence would have developed that could have produced consequences and ramifications way beyond the borders of South Africa. If racism by Europeans and people of European origin or extraction is repugnant, and morally indefensible, then how can racism by nonwhite people against white people be right and defensible?.

Another factor that is catalyzing the quick demise of racism is globalization. For as countries and people become more and more interdependent, economically, linguistically and socially people of different races will intermingle and interact with each other. This process will lead to more inter-racial or biracial marriages or relationships. Although currently, the figures of biracial marriages in Europe, and the Americas are low, the trend is positive. So the more such marriages grow, affecting not only those directly involved, but also their friends and relatives and their supporters, a diminution in racism will occur. For as pointed out earlier, with women being in the majority globally, and as they are not racists themselves, their growing power and influence as mothers, god-mothers, in loco parentis or carers will tend to dampen severely racist views and activities and make them more and more unpopular. This process will hasten the great day that shall surely arrive, when the diminishing bands of racists are reduced to insignificant numbers.

A little true story here may go to elucidate and corroborate the view that more and more biracial marriages or relationships will devastatingly affect racism and quicken its demise. In 1968 at the apogee of racism in the United Kingdom and in Europe and America, with the silent, implied support of many men of God, a prominent high profile British statesman by name Enoch Powell made a public speech in Birmingham, England which was considered by many people as highly inflammatory, racist and unhelpful to good race relations. Many media outlets vigorously supported his right to say what he did, but a few were critical, led by the Guardian, a well-known center left daily newspaper in the United Kingdom. Following this speech, Mr Enoch Powell became very popular on the public lecture circuit and his public persona grew enormously, at least in certain circles.

The leader of the Conservative (Republican) Party in the United Kingdom was so distressed and embarrassed by the speech that he sacked Mr. Enoch Powell from the front bench, (that is the group of members of parliament in the opposition, acting as alternative cabinet, if their party won the next general elections). The bold and principled action of the leader of the party Mr Edward Heath did not dampen in anyway the enthusiasm and popularity of Mr. Powell, who over the years continued to expound and espouse his racist opinions.

Then out of the blue, after several years Mr. Powell publicly recanted and robustly repudiated this speech and the racist views that he had been associated with since the 1968 speech. In 1996 attending a family event with my wife, Breid, at St. Margaret's Church, Westmister Abbey, I was during the recess approached by an elderly, smartly dressed, whitehaired Englishman, who introduced himself to me as Enoch Powell, and shook my hand. To my utter surprise he apologized for that infamous speech and after exchanging a few pleasantries with me, he left. For many months after this encounter,

I still reflected on what must have led to this dramatic change of heart and mind by one of the leading politicians and intellectuals of his generation.

A bigger surprise was to follow. For a few months later watching the BBC Two Television channel in1995 one pleasant night, I saw and heard this outstanding, quintessential English gentleman being interviewed by another Englishman, far younger. And here was Mr Powell not only vigorously denouncing racism but also strongly advocating the ideal of good inter-racial relations in Britain. My wife and I listened completely gob-smacked!!. After getting over the initial shock about what we were seeing and hearing, it took a few minutes to indeed accept that it was not fantasy at all but true. Towards the end of the interview he was asked if was now so opposed to racism and had such strong words against it, what in his opinion was the best way to eradicate it. To his eternal honour, Mr. Enoch Powell stood up to the challenge. I still remember his words indelibly imprinted on my mind. 'Inter-racial marriages, but sadly I do not see many of them about.' I am not in a position to pinpoint when in his life this great man had his dramatic spirtual/intellectual conversion, similar to that of the rabid Jewish anti-Christian, by name Saul, had on his way to Damascus to further his persecution of Jews who had become Christians or wanted to be so. And as some readers may know from the Holy Bible, after his conversion and spiritual rebirth, under the name Paul, he became the greatest evangelist and exponent of Christianity, writing more epistles or letters for the cause and faith than any apostle or disciple of Jesus Christ. Indeed his fervour for his new found faith was such that St. Paul boldly criticized Peter, one of the first and most devoted disciples of Christ. For St. Paul felt that on a number of occasions St. Peter was taking not a bold firm stand in public, but was wishy-washy when confronted by some of the prominent Jewish religious leaders when it came to germane issues of the faith.

The conversion of Mr Enoch Powell from a publicly acclaimed or maligned racist into a robust and fearless adversary of racism and a strong exponent of inter-racial marriages as a means of eliminating racism, remains the enduring legacy of this great Englishman. He saw the light and heard the voice before he went to meet his Maker. Sadly, not many racists are so fortunate, thus dying with their dangerous and immoral ideas and views, with others to unravel the damage that they have caused. I humbly submit that the change of heart and mind of Powell was similar to that of St. Paul and that if Enoch Powell had lived more years after his conversion he would have been a bold and uncompromising challenger or pursuer of racists. Lest the reader is tempted to think that Mr. Powell was an intellectual nonentity I must place on record that he was a highly respected and admired statesman before the sad speech. Before that he had chalked up a good record in the Second World War, had become a university professor of Classics at the incredible age of 23 and was one of the shining lights of post-war British politicians. It is possible that Enoch Powell could have become a prime minister. It is a great shame that many people remember the great man for his infamous speech in 1968 but are completely unaware of his change of heart and mind before he died in 1998. So, William Shakespeare was right when he said in Julius Caesar,'The evil that men do lives after them but the good is often interred with their bones'

It was the spirit of optimism that kept me going when I was in prison in Ghana for fifteen terrible months, and the future looked bleak and daunting. So as an optimist I feel that going by what I term the Enoch Powell Syndrome, even the most rabid racist can at anytime have a dramatic change of heart and conviction and become a strong and unapologetic advocate and exponent of anti-racism to the extent of advancing the cause of inter-racial marriages as one of the effective strategies for combatting the scourge of racism. For I firmly believe that no one is born a racist and that it is the environmental conditions, educational, social, economic and political influences that make them so. People who detest racism should not raise up their arms in despair when they read off and on of a publication by an eminent scientist of international repute who comes out with a statement or book or article that his research has shown that 'black people are inferior or are not as intelligent as Europeans and people of European extraction'. I am sure that given time they would experience the EPS (The Enoch Powell Syndrome) if they are blessed to live a good length of time !.

It is doubtful whether Enoch Powell, whilst publicly advocating inter-racial marriages was aware of the fact that they not only go to challenge and diminish racism, but they also result in some outstanding progeny. And I mention a few here that I am very familiar with. Of course, the argument can be made that biracial marriages fail, or produce people with a propensity for crime or anti-social behavior. True, but such negative attributes and manifestations are not limited to only biracial marriages or partnerships. What about uni-racial or mono-racial marriages which end in divorces, acrimonious or amicable? What about criminals and people of antisocial propensities and activities both of whose parents are or were white? Therefore whether a marriage would fail or succeed or whether children would turn out good citizens or bad depends not on the race of the couple involved but on such factors such as education, proper nutrition, a clean, home or school environment, intellectual stimulation at home, a disciplined and moral upbringing and other factors which have nothing at all whatsoever to do with the race of the parents.

In any case why shouldn't biracial marriages or relationships be allowed to fail or produce undesirable elements just as white/white, or black/black marriages are allowed, or do not cause any stir when they flounder. Indeed, over a period of some decades talking and interviewing many people in Europe and the United States, I have concluded that many white people who appear to show a concern for the future of children of mixed marriages often do as a camouflage for latent racism. For instinctively, I am sure that many of them know that the more of such marriages there are, the quicker would come the elimination of their cherished ideas of racial superiority which they may find inconvenient or inappropriate to express or advance in public. It is true that until the complete eradication of racism the children of such unions can sadly suffer racism, minor or major. However, it is the responsibility of the parents, married or otherwise, to provide the best education, health and other opportunities and facilities for their children so that, fully and appropriately armed and fortified, they can withstand the onslaughts of racism. In effect, as parents of biracial children they must do more for the welfare and life-preparation than would be expected of parents whose children do not encounter or expect to face the scourge of racism. I am happy to state here that I know of many biracial marriages or unions whose children have made a success of their lives and have become good, useful and happy law-abiding citizens, because of the enormous sacrifices that their parents made for their education and welfare. In a good number of cases known to me, the success of the children was such that they were in the financial and economic position to turn the tables on racists or the children of racists, if they so wished.

On the other hand whilst practicing as a lawyer in Accra, Ghana and in my position as deputy minister of health, my attention was drawn to a few cases of physical violence to white women by their African husbands. My anger in all these sad cases derived from my feelings as a human being and as a father, that whatever their excuses or justification for their dreadful acts of violence, they had no legal or moral rights whatsoever to inflict violence on the women. As the women were not their chattels their husbands did not have the right, moral considerations apart, to treat them at their whim and caprice.

Adding to my justified anger was that their behavior unwittingly gave ammunition to the racists waiting in the wings all along to say gleefully, 'We told you so!' The fact that some white men treat badly, with much violence their white wives or partners does not validate the wrongness of the appalling behavior by some black husbands or partners. Compounding the plight of the women is the fact that unlike in Europe and America, there is practically no effective social, safety net for the blighted women to fall into. Indeed, my wife, Breid, with her usual zeal for doing the right thing and standing up for the oppressed and the disadvantaged, irrespective of race, religion or class, turned our home into an unofficial center for battered women to which they brought their diverse and varied conditions. She always treated them very well, listening or having to directly intervene with the misbehaving husbands or having in some cases, left with no alternative, but to give money, food, clothes or organize quick repatriation home of the women. Some even stayed for a couple of nights. Breid did not take a penny from any of the victims of domestic violence nor did she receive any grant or funds from the government. Every expenditure was from her own personal resources, sometimes forced to call on her savings in London.

Aggravating the crimes and unacceptable behaviour of the bad husbands was the fact that in all the cases the women had left their friends and families thousands of miles away to live in a foreign country, under harsh climatic conditions and in a far less developed environment than what they had come from. So whilst there is no excuse or justification for a white man to beat or assault his partner in their home country, the African husband has even far less excuse or justification, to assault his white wife or partner in Africa or for that matter Asia, far away from her original home.

However, in all cases to our knowledge, there was no racial element whatsoever. The men were bad and irresponsible and callous. Their abominable acts of violence derived from the fact that they were bad, and callous, pure and simple, not because they were black. For whilst Breid saw to their suffering and possible amelioration, we knew of many Ghanaian women who were suffering the same plight.

However, the instances of maltreatment of white women by their black husbands were generally the exception to the rule. Most of all the biracial marriages that we were aware of, or acquainted with, were successful. No less successful than occur in Britain and America between white and white couples. As matter of fact, we found over several decades that those involved in biracial marriages usually commit to a determined effort to make a success of the venture. For they are aware and mindful most of the time that they are on a social pedestal, so to speak, being watched much of the time by the public. As they stand out they must, if they have basic humanity, take the responsibility of being in the limelight seriously.

A few instances of the great success of biracial children may be recorded. I am not saying that all biracial children have been successful. Far from it any more than children of parents of the same race are successful or unsuccessful. I am merely stating here that from my experience of over sixty years, through direct observation, discussion, reading and research, I cannot but notice the significant success of such unions, judging by their children. The examples that I refer to are mainly from personal knowledge, especially from Ghana, the African country which has been in the forefront of political, social and economic changes on the great continent for the past sixty years, certainly since the beginning of the 1950's.

First of all, may I humbly remind readers that Alexander Pushkin, the greatest writer and poet of Russia, (the largest country in the world and the most populous in Europe), had genetically African blood coursing in his Russian veins. His maternal great-grand father, Abram Petrovich Gannibal had been either stolen or taken as a seven year old boy probably from Chad or Ethiopia to be a hostage at the court of the Ottoman Sultan. He was ransomed by the Russian Ambassador and taken to the Russian Court of Peter the Great, where he became that famous Emperor's page, confidante and later court official. Pushkin was always proud of his African blood and intended to write a biography on his famous ancestor but was killed in a duel before he had the opportunity. This fact may come as an unpleasant surprise to white racists, who for generations may have revered the outstanding, world famous writer, whilst also blithely traducing black people, as stupid, unintelligent and incapable.

The reason why I have emphasized the successes of the children of biracial marriages is because until only recently biracial unions were illegal and banned in parts of America and most parts of colonial Africa. Such a positive event did not take place in South Africa till 1992. In 1967, the United States Supreme Court unanimously ruled in <u>Loving vs Virginia</u> that anti-miscegenation laws were unconstitutional.

Until fairly recently West Africa, was known in Europe as 'The White man's grave,' and for good reason. Most of the missionaries, traders and adventurers who travelled there either died or did not survive for long under the harsh, hot and humid tropical climate, with no known cures for then prevalent diseases like malaria, cholera, typhoid fever, yellow fever and other insect or water borne diseases. Compounding their plight was the absence of electric fans, let alone air-conditioning. I have visited some of their graves in Accra and Winneba. They all tell their own appallingly tragic stories. Some of the men and women died only a few months after arrival.

Then in 1838 the Methodist Church in England sent a missionary by name, Reverend Thomas Birch Freeman. He settled at Cape Coast and with immense zeal set up a church, schools and the first secondary school in Ghana, Mfantsipim School, the alma mater of the legendary United Nations official and global peacemaker, Kofi Annan. The first English wife of the venerable evangelist, sadly died a few months after arrival, but Thomas Birch Freeman carried on missionary activities to villages nearby and later northwards from his base. He achieved a prodigious amount in in the Gold Coast,(later to be called Ghana, after independence in March 1957).

At a time when the lifespan of most local men was in the forties, due to the unremitting and relentless multipronged onslaughts of pathogenic bacteria and viruses, Reverend Thomas Birch Freeman, who was born in Hampshire, England in 1809 lived to a ripe old age of 81, dying in 1890 in Accra where he is buried. He was unquestionably the greatest of all the missionaries from Europe and England leaving a formidable legacy in Ghana. What is interesting from the point of my submission is that Thomas Birch Freeman was the son of a liberated slave from West Africa, who married a white English maid.

Amazingly, this outstanding evangelist, defying the vicious mosquitoes and flies, carried his work to Benin in Nigeria and to the kingdom of Dahomey, spreading Christ's Word and planting schools in villages and remote places. He resigned from missionary work in 1857 and worked as a civil servant for the Colonial Office in UK, but returned to missionary work in 1873 and continued till his death. Sadly, his two earlier English wives died shortly after arrival but Reverend Thomas Birch Freeman, went on to marry two local women. With one of them he had a son, who carried on with his missionary work after his death. In 1843, while on furlough in Britain, he was active in the anti-slavery cause.*

Due to the fact that in East, Central, North and South Africa during the pre-independence era inter-racial marriages or unions were illegal and not permitted by the colonial powers, which were all white or Caucasian, there were practically none of such marriages. However in West Africa, due to the inclement climate and the malaria and other tropical diseases, there was no desire for white people to settle there. So there was no overt racism, as such, especially regarding biracial marriages. In any case, white people constituted only a tiny fraction of the local population. For example, in my small home town of Agona Swedru,(plus surrounding villages) in the Central Region of Ghana, there were only three white men among about 30,000 indigenous people. In such circumstances it would have been rather unwise and foolhardy for any of the three gentlemen to say or do anything that would incur the wrath of the populace. This is inspite of the visible police protection all drawn from the local community, although paid by their white bosses, as represented by the local district commissioner.

The history and geography of West Africa, in relation to interactions with white people particularly explain why Ghana has relatively high numbers of biracial marriages or unions. Mostly they have been between black men and white women, thus corroborating my earlier assertion or view that white women are not racists. Well, not in any way at all like the men. Although there are many such marriages in Ghana, naturally a few, a small minority have ended in divorce or permanent separation.

The cases of biracial marriages that I have highlighted below are all familiar to me, and my wife, Breid and I have taken a keen interest in them. That in all these cases the marriages have been very successful and the children have been a credit to their parents and nation must to some extent go to support the publicly expressed view of Enoch Powell(a rabid racist turned bold and passionate anti –racist)

---

* (information from Wikipedia)

that inter-racial marriages or unions constitute one of the best, if not the best ways of eliminating racism.

Readers may be interested in a short piece published in the highly respected British Sunday newspaper called The Observer. This is a paper that is greatly admired by millions of educated people in the United Kingdom and in other English-speaking countries. In its edition of 05.07.2015, there was this little gem -

> *"Let's hear for diversity*
> *The results of a vast genetic study, involving 350,000 people and published in Nature show that people whose parents share no identical genes were statistically taller and cleverer than the children of more genetically similar parents. The study might help explain why human beings have become incrementally more intelligent over the past 100 years, as internationally diverse marriages have become more common."*
> <u>So at long last there is good scientific support for inter-racial unions and a scientific explanation why the children of such marriages or unions are exceptionally clever.</u>

**So inter-racial marriages** do not only lead to a diminution of racism but also result in progeny who are taller and cleverer than the usual mono-racial marriages and unions. It is therefore rational to posit that biracial unions are indeed of overall good and benefit to human beings. As such, those who for one reason or another, wittingly or unwittingly, are opposed to them, privately or publicly, are in effect retarding the progress of mankind. It is debatable whether their activities, meant or expected, to lead to a slowing down in interracial unions rise to the level of constituting 'crimes against humanity' and thus requiring an investigation by the International Criminal Court at the Hague, The Netherlands. I am sure that the list below is not comprehensive, but a mere snippet of these marriages but they should serve the purpose that I am endeavoring to advance here, namely that biracial unions are a positive good for mankind at large.

## 1.  OBETSEBI FAMILY:

Mr Obetsebi Lamptey, went to England in the early -forties, where he studied law and was called to the English Bar. He was one of the Big Six-the first six nationalist leaders to be imprisoned by the British colonial power in the early stages of the anti-colonial struggle against British rule. He married a Dutch woman and their son, Jake, became a highly respected and formidable statesman in Ghana. Before that he had built a successful career as a media/public relations consultant. Went on to shine as a government minister in Ghana under the presidency of John Agyekum Kufuor, 2001-2009

## 2.  THE JOE APPIAH SAGA

The marriage in 1953 of Joe Appiah, then a law student/anti-colonial activist and Hyde Park orator to Peggy Cripps, the daughter of the legendary Sir Stafford Cripps, the British, postwar chancellor of the Exchequer of Britain that is, Secretary of Treasury(US) or Finance Minister, deserves special mention. In 1951 Joe Appiah who was at the end of his law studies in London, during which period he had been a vocal and public campaigner for colonial independence, got married at St. Martin's-In-the-Fields Church at Trafalgar Square, London.

Peggy Cripps had met the vibrant and articulate West African at one of his frequent talks at the West African Students Union, a modest building near the famous Harrods store in London. The romance bloomed and Joe Appiah was invited to the Cripps home, off and on. When Peggy made her intentions known to her parents, according to reliable accounts, they advised her to visit the Gold Coast. She did, staying with Mr and Mrs. Kojo Botsio in Accra. Kojo, a close friend of both Joe Appiah and Kwame Nkrumah, was at that time the Minister for Education, in the newly formed government, led by Kwame Nkrumah. During her stay, Peggy Cripps went to

Kumasi, Joe's hometown in the Ashanti region, and met friends and relatives of Joe Appiah and others, including the Asantehene (king).

She returned home to London still resolved to go ahead. So with the blessing of her mother (as her father had passed away), the historic wedding took place, attended by the high and mighty, the great and the good of the post war Labour Government. The event received comprehensive media attention in London, with the largest selling daily newspaper in the world at the time, the Daily Mirror giving it a full front page photographic coverage. At a time in Europe and Britain when racism was part of normal life, private and public, with even men of God turning a blind eye to it and its victims, the wedding and the accompanying huge publicity caused a scandal, a veritable cause celebre, and had a seismic effect on race relations. For here was the daughter of one of the best educated and respected families in Great Britain, the 'Mother Country', as she was known throughout the Empire, marrying a 'blanket clad native' as the newspaper derisively dubbed Joseph's expensive, hand woven kente* cloth apparel. To add insult to injury, as the racists saw it, the bride was tall, elegant, pretty, intelligent and educated. Compounding the distress and anger of the racists was the fact that Joe Appiah was a recently qualified English barrister, from an established, prosperous home in West Africa and related to the local Royal Family.

The extent of the damage that the wedding did to the ego and stance of white supremacy in Europe and Africa can be gauged by this incident. The prime minister of South Africa was so incensed with what their kith and kin had done in London that during a debate in parliament, he furiously waved a copy of the Daily Mirror before his all-white assembly, who were collectively unable to control their sheer anger.

After the wedding, the Appiahs settled comfortably and well in KUMASI, THE CAPITAL OF THE Ashanti Region. There for

---

* Kente is the traditional grand occasion attire (akin to tuxedo or tail coat) in Ghana

several years the couple looked after their children and entertained, as befitted their elevated position in the local community.

Many went to their home out of sheer curiosity, but others from Britain had good journalistic reasons to see how the celebrated daughter of Sir Stafford Cripps was fairing. Consistently, the news was not what racists wanted to hear or read! For apart from brief vacation visits to England, Peggy Appiah spent all her life in Kumasi. She was a most amiable hostess, as many visitors including my wife and I can attest.

Immersing herself in the study of her husband's culture and the language of the Ashantis, she wrote books on it and gave talks also. The Appiahs had three children. The eldest, Kwame Appiah, Cambridge University educated became one of the most eminent professors in America, holding professorships at Harvard, Princeton and New York. Additionally he has held professorships in other countries. Apart from being an accomplished writer, he has won numerous awards, including the Medal of Honor in the USA. Of the two daughters, one trained and qualified as a lawyer in Britain, married a Norwegian shipping tycoon and settled comfortably in Norway. Joe Appiah died in Accra in 1990, aged 71.

The other daughter stayed with her parents, assisting her mother in her study and voluntary work among the Ashantis. Mrs Peggy Appiah died in Kumasi in 2006, aged 84. That the president of Ghana, John Agyekum Kufuor wrote a special obituary on Peggy Appiah is only one of the many indications of the great admiration, love and respect that this outstanding, highly principled daughter of the United Kingdom was held in the hearts of the people of Ghana and other parts of Africa.

## 3. THE PIANIM FAMILY

Andrew Kwame PIANIM, a celebrated economist/statesman was born in Ghana, educated at the prestigious boarding school, Achimota and then at universities in Canada and the United States of America. He received outstanding post graduate degrees and married a Dutch woman, Cornelia, with whom he had three children –two boys and a girl. Their son, Elkin, trained as a corporate financier and married Elizabeth Murdock, the daughter of one of the greatest media moguls in the world. The wedding in California was attended by some of the great and the good of the only super-power on earth, including Dr. Henry Kissinger and former president Ronald Reagan and wife. The glittering wedding in1992 in California was as historic as that of Joe Appiah to Peggy Cripps, referred to above. The Pianim daughters became a doctor in America.

This wedding must have given racists a lot to ponder over. For like Peggy Cripps in 1953, here was the beautiful, bright and Vassar educated daughter of one of the wealthiest and most influential men in the world marrying a black man, albeit half -white. And to cap it all, the bride was the personification of brains and beauty. She, later in life, established an enviable and stellar reputation in the media in her own right, earning a mention in the Sunday Times annual RICH LIST, which requires a minimum of one hundred million pounds sterling (US$155.00 million) in assets to qualify for entry!

## 4.   THE HEWARD-MILLS FAMILY

Barrister Nathaniel Heward-Mills was born of an established Royal Family in the Ga tribe, who are concentrated around Accra. He studied law and was called to the English Bar. In England he married a Swiss woman, Elizabeth, and they had two children. The eldest, a boy Dag, originally wanted to be a doctor but at the last stage of his medical education had a call from God, experiencing a religious rebirth. Answering the higher call to give up his life in the service of God, he terminated his studies and became an evangelist. Against all odds he established his own church, the Lighthouse Chapel International. In a relatively short time it grew and expanded rapidly in Ghana, with demands for his religious services emanating from various parts of the world. Currently he is bishop of his Charismatic church, has written several books and given talks, seminars and sermons in many countries in Asia, Africa and the Caribbean. In the very competitive field of global evangelization, with numerous apostles, prophets and growing at an exponential rate, with their accompanying churches and tabernacles, the rapid success world wide of Bishop Dag Heward-Mills has been outstanding by any measure.

## 5.  THE BUTAH FAMILY

Captain Joseph K. Butah, born in Ashanti and trained as a naval officer in Britain under a scholarship programme funded by the Nkrumah Government. He married Glenda chivers, a Welsh woman and they have three children. The eldest, a son, became an officer in the British army, reaching the rank of major. He served with distinction in Afghanistan and Iraq and was the first coloured or black officer to command the Trooping of the Color, the prestigious annual event in London, hosted by HER MAJESTY THE QUEEN. After an exemplary military service, he left and is now the CEO of the security division of a large, international oil company in Accra. Of his two sisters, the elder has an excellent degree in econometrics, apart from acheiving considerable success as a singer/song-writer and the other is a lawyer.

## 6.  HANNAH TETTEH

Hannah Serwaa Tetteh is a highly respected lawyer/stateswoman who was born in Hungary, is a true combination of brains and beauty. She is a Member of Parliament and currently Foreign Minister (Secretary of State) of Ghana. She was previously the Minister for Trade and Industry. In a country where frequently rumors circulate about corruption among politicians, her reputation has solidly stood intact and unblemished. Her father was a Ghanaian doctor who trained in Hungary, and her mother was a Hungarian doctor. This fine lady is a credit to interracial marriage. Hannah Serwaa Tetteh is the first woman foreign minister of Ghana in a non-military, democratically elected government.

## 7.  PRESIDENT JERRY RAWLINGS

This remarkable, controversial and formidable man is hated by many Ghanaians for his record in politics but hugely admired by many others. Born in Ghana of a Scottish father and a Ghanaian mother, Flight Lieutenant Jerry Rawlings attended the prestigious government boarding school in Ghana called Achimota School. He was an ace pilot in the Ghana Air force before leading a violent coup in June 1979. Whether he is liked or not, his record of ruling Ghana for almost twenty years, both as a military dictator and later as a democratically elected civilian president cannot be ignored. June-September 1979 saw him as head of a violent military junta. Then in his second comeback in Dec.31, 1981—2000, first as a military dictator and later as a benign, democratically elected Head of State. He continues to cast a heavy presence and influence on the politics of Ghana since handing over to President John Agyekum Kufuor in January 2001. As a result of the hundreds of people who were killed by the military and their agents during his rule, many of his detractors cite him as not the ideal product of inter-racial relationships. Married into one of the greatest Ashanti families, ex-president Rawlings has three daughters and a son. His preparedness to willingly give up power as a military dictator and metamorphose into a civilian democratic Head of State was to his abiding credit. It is interesting to note that since leaving office, he has been a bold and stout supporter of democratic governance and fierce opponent of bribery and corruption.

## 8.   KOFI ANNAN AND FAMILY

One of the most outstanding Africans of the twenty-first century, excluding Madiba Nelson Mandela, he will ever be remembered as one of the greatest international public servants. Born in Ghana, after a solid Methodist education, he had a good university education in the USA and CANADA. Kofi joined the fledgling Ghana diplomatic service in 1960, then served in the United Nations rising to become secretary general from 1997 until 2006. Even in active retirement has not only set up a foundation to promote world peace and development, but he is frequently sought after as an international arbiter or negotiator, which is a reflection of the stellar qualities and attributes of this great man He has a good record as a philanthropist

Married for the second time to a tall, beautiful and bright lawyer to the UN from Sweden, Nane Lagergren, since 1984 their marriage has amply corroborated the growing evidence that biracial marriages do work well and go to support the view of Enoch Powell that they contribute to the eradication of racism. Readers may be interested to know that this fine and elegant lady is the niece of the legendary Swedish diplomat in Budapest by name Rauol Wallenberg who, during the Second World War, saved thousands of Jews in Hungary when they faced imminent death by issuing them with Swedish passports. This noble and altruistic act of his swiftly facilitated their flight to Sweden, thus saving their lives. Sadly Raoul Wallenberg disappeared in January 1945 following the capture of Budapest by the invading Soviet forces. He is presumed to have been killed in a Russian prison. The Wallenbergs are among the wealthiest and most respected families in Sweden. By the late 1990s the Wallenbergs controlled 40% of the value of companies listed on the Swedish Stock Exchange. Sweden is a relatively small country which has for decades made exemplary, outstanding and disproportionately immense contributions to global peace, harmony and the causes of humanity.

## 9.  THE SERETSE KHAMA SAGA

In 1921, Seretse Khama, was born into the Rroyal Family of then Bechuanaland, a British protectorate. He was a law student in England when he met and married a Welsh woman, Ruth Williams in London in 1948. The neighboring apartheid government of South Africa was outraged by the biracial marriage and threatened to take action. Caving under pressure, the socialist government in Great Britain at the time needed cheap South African gold and uranium, and so banned him from returning to his country of birth. Socialist principles were thrown out of the window along with the brotherhood of man, and egalitarianism was trampled on as the British Government gave into South African demands.

The controversy ignited by this very inhuman decision raged for many months. In 1956 the couple were allowed to return to his country, but only after he had renounced any claim to the throne. Subsequently, he became involved in politics, then formed his own party and won elections, becoming Prime Minister in 1965. Then in 1966 with the country gaining independence from Britain, Seretse Khama, was elected first President of the newly named Republic of Botswana. He governed his country well and properly, leading to its rapid development in education, infrastructure and the quality of life of the people. He died in 1980 at the age of 59. He and Ruth had a daughter and three sons. His son, Ian followed the father's footsteps and became the president in 2009 while his brother Tshekedi was elected as a parliamentarian.

## 10. JOMO KENYATTA

Born in Kenya in 1891 he went to London as a student and trained as an anthropologist and wrote several books and was active in the anti-colonialist movement in London. He married an Englishwoman in 1942. She was his second wife, but the marriage did not endure. Their son Peter Kenyatta, born in the United Kingdom in 1943 became a well-known and popular BBC presenter and producer until retiring. Jomo Kenyatta returned to his homeland and led the independence movement which achieved victory in 1963 He was President from Dec.1964 till his death in Nairobi, Kenya in Aug.1978 at the age of 86. He is revered as the founding father of independent Kenya.

## 11. LORD PAUL BOATENG

This remarkable man had a Ghanaian father (a British-trained barrister) and a Scottish mother, a teacher. Born in Hackney, London in June 1951, his father, Kwaku Boateng and his family moved to Ghana in 1953 where he became one of the outstanding members of the government of Dr. Kwame Nkrumah. In 1966, following the military overthrow of the Nkrumah Government in February 1966 and his arrest and imprisonment, without trial the family returned to the United Kingdom with his younger sister, Rosemary, later a teacher. Paul was an exceptional student, who trained first as a solicitor and later as a barrister. Like president Barack Obama, Paul Boateng, immersed himself in community work and helped many people, especially the socially or racially disadvantaged. He joined the British Labour Party (The Democratic Party) and became a member of Parliament and then the first mixed race cabinet minister in British history. He concluded his public career as ambassador to South Africa. Paul Boateng was made a member of the House of Lords (U.K's unelected Second Chamber, akin to the US Senate).

The list above admittedly is not detailed or comprehensive. There are millions of such remarkable stories all over the world, particularly in America, Canada and Europe. But I hope that this list, short as it, demonstrates the achievements of biracial marriages and their children, give an inkling of what biracial marriages and unions can do towards the elimination of racism. Furthermore they show that the fears expressed in the early 1950's by some white people that biracial marriages should not be encouraged because the children would suffer were completely unfounded. For all the people mentioned above have in one way or another endured racism. This includes even the most recent of them all, President Barack Obama. So if despite racism, covert or overt, mild or severe, these people have chalked up such remarkable records in spite of the disadvantages they endured then surely there is a compelling case for biracial marriages and unions.

Often the argument is made by many white people that 'Poilitcal Correctness has gone mad' if people cannot freely criticize in public the words and deeds of self-appointed anti-racists who sometimes get carried away by their zeal to see 'the right thing done'. These people may not be racists themselves, but in a charged atmosphere, they may be made to appear so. However, whilst I fully agree with their right to exercise their human rights, including free speech, I am of the considered opinion that a line needs to be drawn somewhere. This is not because there is a desire to curb their rights but because human experiences over thousands of years have amply demonstrated that unless there are such reasonable and justifiable limits to the expression or exercise of legitimate human rights the result is anarchy.

To take an example from the lives and activities of primates, of which the Human being is the highest. All primates, including even our nearest cousins, the Bonono monkeys, eat, drink, rest and perform normal excretory functions when they feel like it, at any time, anywhere, without any inhibitions at all whatsoever. But human beings over thousands of years have learnt that such a lifestyle is in not conducive to the public good, nor indeed even for the best interest of the individual. So in all communities, including the simplest, laws or rules have been introduced regulating or limiting, in a way, when, where, and even how all these vital bodily functions averred to above can be performed. All rational people accept that these limitations on our freedoms, or human rights are necessary and good for the survival, wellbeing and happiness of all of us. Well at least for the vast majority. And it would be no defence for a man found standing in the public square robustly spewing out obscene language against some of the revered institutions of his society to say that he was mearly exercising his human rights. Most likely passersby would request him to stop and if he does not they may call in the police. When the police on arrival ask him to stop but he still continues maintaining that he is merely exercising his human rights, he would be taken away to a police station. There, if he still insists that he was right in the exercise of human rights and is not prepared to apologize he would be cautioned, then charged and later put before a court. There his plea of human rights not withstanding he would be either reprimanded, or convicted and given a fine or possibly a stint in prison.

Even in the poorest developing countries, this is the procedure for those who want to exercise their human rights to the fullest extent, oblivious of the consequences of such actions on others. For as other human beings in the same society or community or country they owe a responsibility to them.

Admittedly in many developing countries regulations or laws meant to stop or prevent environmental degradation or unnecessary assaults by individuals or groups may not be rigorously or firmly implemented. But they do exist as the ideal to pursue or aim at. So whilst fully accepting that all human beings have the right as human beings to do or say or write or act as they feel like, surely there must be limits otherwise jungle law or mobocracy will prevail and not democracy. And over thousands of years human experience has shown that democracy is the best form or system of governance for human beings. For it ensures that all human beings are free to enjoy their human rights equitably, fairly and reasonably, and not at the expense of others.

I have been privileged in my life to live in democratic countries. I have also travelled extensively in many countries in Europe, Asia and America where democracy is the accepted form of governance. I have also experienced life in a communist country and lived under brutal, military regimes in Africa. So my commitment to free exercise of human rights is not at all academic but the result of personal, hard-earned experiences over several decades. And it is precisely as a result cumulatively of these experiences over at least sixty years that I have come to the firm conclusion that it is not 'Political correctness gone mad 'when racists or their apologists or supporters are requested for the common good and communal peace to tone down their rhetoric, at least in public.

Likewise it is incumbent on all sides of every argument and debate to do the same. Off course, in the privacy of their homes or private clubs what people say or do viz-a viz racism, or any other policy issue, is entirely their own business. No one should deny them that right But it is an entirely different proposition, when they insist on behaving or saying in public all that they are fully entitled to do in private, without any limitations whatsoever. For that is a perfect recipe for needless oral confrontations that may easily escalate into physical violence, with a high risk of injuries or even fatalities. Any person who thinks that such a scenario is in the best interest of human societies can hardly be called a true friend of mankind .

It is true that great strides have been taken to outlaw, deride and eliminate racism. More still needs to be achieved. However, because the issue is a political hot potato, people can use the label of racism as a means to attack an opponent, much as today, many people are tempted to call anyone who disagrees with them 'a Nazi'.

So it is incumbent upon us all, that we not only talk in generalities but that we provide facts and proofs for our arguments, not empty, emotionally-charged rhetoric which beneath its apparent noble intention masks a thrust for power.

To recapitulate, may I state that this work is meant to encourage a healthy dialogue between racists and their victims. For racism is a serious problem that should concern all who love humanity and want to live in a world where achievements, opportunities in life depend not on skin colour, but on what the individual, as an individual, really is. Any attempt to structure national policies on the basis of race is not only wrong morally, but is also bound to have deleterious effects on the perpetrators. For they cannot escape the consequences of their actions. Therefore, although at present and for the past four centuries, Europeans and peoples of European descent have benefitted enormously, politically, economically and socially from racism, recent history has amply demonstrated that the roles can be reversed any time. The demise of apartheid in South Africa should serve as a warning and a lesson to racists. Moral considerations apart, it is simply not in the enlightened best interest of white people to support, condone or actively promote racism. I refer here to white people as perpetrators of racism because to date it is they who have been in the economic or political position to indulge in this baneful ideology, although I am well aware that all humans have the trait of being suspicious and fearful of the outsider. No doubt in the past it helped us to survive, but now it generally leads to animosity, unfair discrimination and even war.

Furthermore as the history of fascism in Germany, Italy and Japan has shown, racism, if not nipped in the bud but allowed to bloom and flourish, can put into the heads and hearts of national leaders fanciful and grotesque ideas, whose implementation bring untold catastrophe and unimaginable destruction and deaths on the perpetrators and their innocent victims. A careful reading of a few of the major books on World War 2, coupled with serious study of the renowned television documentaries on the war clearly show that there was simply no realistic way the three Axis Powers (Germany

Italy Japan) could bring to fruition their racist ambitions of global conquest and domination.

I am of the firm view that racism can easily be uprooted from the world. With globalization and the galloping rate in communication among nations and peoples, the fear, ignorance and bigotry underpinning this heinous ideology will rapidly disappear. In any case, the growing industrial development and advancement in Asia, the Middle East, Africa and the Caribbean region will impact negatively on this ideology that has caused the world much pain and suffering. The world has so much unexploited resources, natural, mineral and others that there is simply no need for fears by any groups that they would starve or perish and need to ensure against such a calamity by trying to dominate others. The seas, land, on the ground and in the deep bowels of the earth, are teeming with abundant resources, waiting to be tapped and developed for the benefit of mankind. And ideologies and practices such as racism simply detract human beings from fully engaging in utilizing all the resources around us.

To expedite the end of racism, a global challenge, all human beings have a role to play. This may be done at the individual level, at the family level and at the work place or entertainment venue.

For instance, if a white father gets used to making racist remarks or jokes at home to the delight of his children, but the mild disapproval of the wife then he should not be at all surprised if ten, fifteen or twenty years later one of the sons gets into trouble with the police for allegedly making a racist remark in public. Who is to blame? Worse, if the son, who is bright, intelligent with a good future, inadvertently says something or behaves in a way deemed racist in any country where non Europeans are in the majority and in control of the levers of power, and is arrested and following prosecution he receives a stiff prison sentence (devoid of the lovely meals, color television, comfortable bed, exercise facilities, library, etc), during which time he may expect unwelcome visits from uninvited flies and mosquitoes, who is to blame for his predicament? Wouldn't the unfortunate son in his dire predicament be right to blame his parents, especially the father for his sad situation?

Let's consider another not all that hypothetical a situation. Daddy, in his mid-forties and doing well at work, awash with knowledge, ideas and talent, expecting imminent promotion. in a moment of forgetfulness, makes a racist remark that goes viral. He is suspended, pending an investigation by the senior managers. After the process of enquiry he is found culpable and is dismissed from his job. Who is accountable for the tragic development? Even if he is reinstated,(following profuse and humiliating apologies in public) rather unlikely, yet what about the loss in reputation, with repercussions on the family, who used to enjoy his jokes? There are numerous scenarios taking place in America and Europe which suggest that excluding the moral dimension of racism, the practice at least in public is not in the best enlightened interest of white men who gaily indulge in it.

Of course, the diehard racist can argue that Europeans and those of European origins can do without the rest. But this is palpably not so. It is as false a claim as saying that the shop-keeper can do without the shoppers and vice-versa. In any case, the history of the world shows that societies that lived or tried to live in blissful isolation, ended over hundreds of years by going extinct.

In an article I read a few years ago in the highly respected time magazine, the author convincingly established that the greatness of the United States of America is due to immigration and innovation. for the former brings in new blood, continually refreshing the gene pool, which leads to greater creativity, productivity, and better quality of life. Little wonder that starting as a group of 13 struggling colonies in the eighteenth century that country in a matter of a few decades has become the richest and most powerful in the history of the world, with its economic and political power extending far beyond its own borders and affecting peoples of all races and nationalities.

Admittedly, racism, even without the active intervention of campaigners against it, is on a downward trajectory, as a result of forces that even incorrigible racists cannot control. But what the campaigns against racism do is to accelerate the coming demise of the dangerous ideology and practice. For its survival, day by day, produces deleterious effects, economic, political, and social on its victims. The indirect results of racism on its perpetrators, or active apologists, are becoming rather expensive and making the practice or advocacy of racism rather counter-productive. Already, many major corporations, universities, research centres, sports and entertainment organisations in America and the United Kingdom, are finding that an employee or colleague who is exposed in public as a racist is a liability. And in each and every case of such exposure there is a dramatic drop in his friends and supporters, even if privately they may share some or all of his views!

It needs be recorded that even in the United States of America, with all the sad and deplorable cases of the shooting of unarmed black men by white police men, the trajectory of racism is on the descent. For these sad instances of the use of excessive force against unarmed men, whatever may be the explanation or justification, can only accentuate race relations not for the better, but for the worse. On the other hand, there are many good policemen who are now coming under unwarranted attack themselves because of people inciting hatred against them and it has been the case that crimes have gone unattended by the police, because of their recent vulnerability.

Furthermore, these episodes and other forms of racism, still manifest in the country and widely publicized by the American and world media, go to tarnish the great image and name worldwide of the United States of America as the bastion of freedom and democracy and the world's guarantor of peace and democracy.

At the risk of being considered naïve or stupid, I state that it is indeed the rapid downward trend in racism in America that made it possible on two historic occasions for Barack Obama(called black although half white) to be elected president of America, by voters who were preponderantly white. For if the white voters, about 65%, had played the race card, and prioritized the candidate's skin color above all other considerations, issues and factors in the elections how could he win, if even all the African-Americans, Hispanics, Native Americans mixed race and other minorities voted for him? What is clear from his election is that the majority of voters in the US are <u>not</u>

racist. And many who did not vote for him are not racist either, but disagreed with his policies.

It is for the common good, as we all live in the same global village, that we make our contributions however modest to the eradication of racism. And I trust that I have made a case for the benefits of a society or world which is rid of racism.

But after over six decades active involvement in the cause of antiracism I must sound a word of warning in what I perceive as the deplorable instances of growing racism in reverse in some countries in Africa and Asia, and other parts of the globe, predominantly inhabited or controlled by non-Europeans. The temptation of some educated people in positions of power, albeit a very tiny minority, in these countries to want to practice racism in reverse is totally wrong and deserves to be condemned robustly, and without fear or favor.

For if racism by white people against nonwhite people is wrong morally and a gross travesty against justice, fairness and human dignity, then how can it be right when non-Europeans racially discriminate against white people? Do two wrongs make a right? How or why should Asians and Africans fight racism with racism, when there are more refined, sophisticated and civilized strategies, processes and mechanisms available?.

Just as I have firmly condemned racism by white people whenever and wherever possible, I have equally done so when the baneful ideology has reared its ugly head in Ghana or parts of the world where I have seen it. For it is precisely because the ideology is bad, evil, repugnant and immoral that we should all help to end it. And this must include even those who have been victims of it, either as individuals or as nations. Otherwise, we would, by our inaction expose ourselves as not only immoral or amoral, but also as having failed to learn from history, especially the recent past.

This book is not meant to be an academic treatise, not at all. It is meant to be a conversation or dialogue with all people who view racism as evil and wrong and feel or wish to do something positive to bring it to an end. As such, my personal experiences and those of others known to me, plus accounts and reports that I have read are germane to this conversation. It is in this vein that I narrate here a true story in my own life relevant to this dialogue. For it demonstrates that Africans or Asians in positions of influence or power can rise above the harmful ideology and deal or treat people not on the basis of their skin colour but for what they are or do.

In November 1961, after four happy and enjoyable years in London, first as a journalist and later as a diplomat at the Ghana Embassy (High Commission) I was appointed an ambassador at the age of 28, then one of the youngest in the world. After the routine diplomatic orientation course in Ghana in late 1961, I took up my appointment in Budapest as my country's first ambassador to Hungary and the International Atomic Energy Agency, Vienna, Austria. Before leaving I had been fortunate to meet with a bright and beautiful and sharp-witted Irish woman, of impeccable qualities. At a time when racism was rife and was at its apogee, in private and public life in the United Kingdom, connived at or condoned by powerful men of God, she had boldly stood up against racism, not only privately but publicly.

Her brave and principled stance had earned her a few nasty telephone calls and a rude graffiti on her window. For she had given accommodation to a troupe of dancers and singers from apartheid South Africa who had been ejected from their London hotel for making noise during rehearsals! But Breid's anti-racism stand had also brought her to the attention of the Ghana Government in Accra and the Ghana Embassy in London. She was subsequently visited and thanked by the embassy chaplain on behalf of the Ghana Governement and the embassy. I was then instructed as public relations advisor to go and interview this outstanding white woman who had stood up for black people when even religious men were silent or deaf to the racial injustice prevailing.

This great, beautiful and very bright Jewish, British, Irish woman, running her own restaurant in London was later to become my wife for over 53 years (and still going strong). But before the happy event a bizzare situation arose. For as required by the rules of our foreign ministry (department), I wrote to the foreign minister or secretary of state, for permission to marry a non-national. This was a procedure that the country had inherited from our British colonial administration before independence in March 1957.

To my utter surprise whilst in Vienna attending a conference at the International Atomic Energy agency, as Ghana's ambassdador I received a call from the Daily Express newspaper in London. The caller identified himself as a writer for the William Hickey Column of the paper. He said that my permission to marry had been refused by the foreign minister. Naturally, I was rather puzzled and taken aback, as I had not received the said letter.

A few days later the diplomatic bag arrived and when I received the letter, the contents were as my caller had said. It took me a few days to get over the shock but I decided that on principle I must fight to the very end, if it even meant losing my hugely comfortable job, with all the perks, and enormous salary! For the refusal to my request was on 'security grounds'. I felt that the grounds for the action by my boss were ridiculous and specious and at heart, racist. It was 'racism' camouflaged as 'national security concerns' and I was determined to expose it for what it was.

So I wrote a polite but well-argued case to the foreign minister in which I stated that his concerns were completely unfounded, as I did not deal with any security matters, nor handle the code book or was in any way associated with any foreign intelligence agency. I also drew to his attention the strong and public stand of my fiancé against racism, which had received the commendation and gratitude of the Ghana Government and embassy in London. Privately, I felt that as Ghana was only emerging from colonial rule under the British and was grossly in hock to Britain and her friends it was fanciful to think that if even independent Ghana had any secrets at all, atomic, economic or political, Britain and other powers could not lay their hands on them, if they so wished.

Furthermore, I knew too well that we had no secrets, particularly atomic. For our fledgling atomic energy programme was in its very infancy. And any important financial or economic data and information were known to British sources, on which the Ghana

Government relied upon principally. Even the Code Book that we used at the embassy was from the British! In any case, the Osagyefo (meaning The Great Warrior or Commander or Leader) the President himself was married to a foreigner. With all these considerations flowing through my mind I was certain that my appeal would not fail. For it passed the test of reason, at least from my humble point of view. On principle, although a Crown or kingdom was not at stake I had decided to resign and damn the consequences, if my request was not granted.

Fortunately for me, a few weeks after my letter I had to go to Ghana in connection with the preparations for the pending first official visit of the prime minister of Hungary.

A day or two after my arrival in Accra I made enquiries about my appeal at the foreign ministry. The position had not changed but not worsened either. So a couple of days after the highly successful visit by the Hungarian prime minister and his delegation, I called the cabinet secretary and requested an appointment with the Osagyefo himself to appeal to him directly. A week later, one cool morning I was called to the Flagstaff House (Ghana's White House or 10, Downing Street) in Accra. Sitting timidly before the great man, who for the past fifteen years had been engrossed in the struggle against colonialism, and apartheid, I literally trembled, although I tried to put on a warm smile. For here was the man who was then spearheading the freedom movements in East, Central and South Africa and had been sending clandestinely funds, weapons and other forms of assistance to those in Africa who unlike Ghana were still not free from white colonial rule or from apartheid, the cruel and vile form of racism by a small, white minority against a huge, black majority.

Additionally, the Osagyefo himself had, according to his oral and written accounts, suffered terrible racism during his twelve years stay in America, and later a similar two year spell in England. To compound my predicament, the foreign minister was a close personal friend from their student days in America. Was he going to allow his bitter personal experiences and avowed stance against white racism to tempt him to do racism in reverse? As I sat plaintively before him I speculated what was in store for me. Was this going to be the end of my great and luxurious life as ambassador? Suddenly, talking rather fast, Osagyefo said and I recall his words very well right to this day. 'I saw the memo from Foreign Affairs but I did not mind them. In this world it is the <u>person</u> that counts, not his skin colour'. I sighed with relief!. Then jokingly he added, 'Go ahead, and don't forget to send me a piece of the wedding cake !'.

In a matter of a few minutes my ordeal was over and I was over the moon, almost delirious with happiness. The response of the president of Ghana, the Osagyefo Dr. Kwame Nkrumah to my humble request had amply demonstrated that even victims of racism can show a better example by not being racist, whatever the temptation and urge. Readers can therefore understand why I always feel so sad when I read or hear of white high profile men or people in positions of power or influence allegedly making racist remarks or exhibiting racist behavior. For they appear oblivious of the fact that not only is racism wrong and immoral but that it is a double –edged sword. For as the people in Asia, the Pacific Region, the Middle East and Africa, and other lands outside Europe and America, become better organized, better educated, disciplined and industrialized some of their leaders can, if they so wish, also indulge in racism. Of course it would be entirely wrong and only serve to perpetuate the cycle of racism and further racism ! And I would be failing completely in my moral duty as a human being, blessed with several happy and comfortable years on this earth if I condone or connive at racism by nonwhite people against white people. The job is not completely done unless I actively join in enlightening, persuading or cajoling racists that their stance is not only wrong but carries with it the potential risk of creating in the long term, unnecessary misery and suffering for innocent white people. Furthermore, that history is not on their side and what they perceive now to be a social or political or economic advantage may not turn out to be so, a few decades later.

A little true story here may serve to illustrate how nonwhite people sometimes are tempted to play the race card, if they feel doing so would be to their advantage. Following my release from fifteen months imprisonment without trial, in Accra, Ghana in March 1973 I resumed practice as a lawyer. Practically all my clients were Europeans or Americans. I am sure that they came to me not because I was the leading legal luminary, nor because my fees were low but because they felt or knew from the grape vine that I would fight in their corner right to the end, without fear or favour. This is no exaggerated claim at all, as they can easily attest, or others may verify. Where and when I felt that my own compatriots were being racist I told them in no uncertain terms, even at the risk of being considered by some as naïve or worse as a white boot-licker or victim of a brainwash! For I felt that having in all my adult life been active in fighting racism, I simply could not stand aside, deaf and blind, when I encountered it even among my fellow compatriots.

Another pertinent story here may go to corroborate my point that there are indeed some cases, albeit few where there has been racism in reverse. After my release from prison, whilst practicing as a lawyer, my dear wife, Breid got me involved in a case of a biracial marriage. A handsome, tall Englishman had married an attractive Ghanaian woman, and after that had sent her to the United Kingdom to train as a beautician. Subsequently they had two gorgeous children, a boy and a girl. About fourteen years after the wedding, the couple divorced. The divorce settlement by a Ghanaian, British trained lawyer/judge, applying principles of English matrimonial law gave the family car, the smartly furnished home and contents to the wife. Also a substantial lump sum payment was given her. Additionally, the father was to pay for the upkeep and education of the children till adulthood, with shared access to the children. By any yardstick the settlement was very fair and equitable to the wife. Next starts the episode. Urged on by her Ghanaian boy-friend or partner, the woman was determined to pursue her claim to half of their home in a salubrious part of England.

Quietly but firmly I advised her that her claim was unreasonable, that she already had received a fair settlement and that no court on the facts of the case would agree to her request. During at least two sessions I tried to let her see reason. Her expectation of me as a fellow

Ghanaian to be on her side, expressed clearly by body language, cut no ice with me. Spurred on by her new man and evidently infected by the virus of greed, she spurned and rejected my advice. I made it clear to Mrs. X that if I were the English judge hearing the case, I would without hesitation reject her claim. Finally, I advised her again to reconsider her position. Then we parted company amicably.

About fifteen months later I learnt from Breid, who had been instrumental in my involvement in the case on a 'pro bono' basis that the woman had died in the United Kingdom. Apparently, after she and her partner left Breid and me, they had gone to England and hired expensive lawyers to fight her case. Unsurprisingly, she had lost. For the English judge had ruled that following the Ghana settlement, there was no merit in her claim to any rights or share in the home in England. The shock to her had been such that she had shortly suffered a severe nervous breakdown, which had led to her hospitalization. Her condition deteriorated rapidly, as other post traumatic illnesses followed and despite all the best efforts of the doctors she was dead in a few months. So, consumed by greed, fueled by racism and given the oxygen of support by her partner she had taken a stance that had led to her early and unnecessary death at about forty, leaving two orphans Their sad predicament was not caused by an accident or a degenerative disease such as cancer but by the folly, stubbornness, greed and racism of an otherwise fine woman who refused to take advice offered on a nonracist basis.

Another personal story may be appropriate here, to emphasis how the usual scenario of black people being helped by white people may be reversed. One evening when returning home from work in Budapest, Hungary, I noticed that a group of people were excitedly hovering over an injured person. I instructed my chauffeur to stop and I walked to the spot. It was an old woman who had been seriously injured in a car accident. As my interpreter/translator was not with me, I could not understand fully what they were saying. But I caught the words, 'fekete'(meaning black or black man) and 'najkovet' (ambassador) and 'hospital'. The situation was rather desperate. So I immediately asked them to put the lady in my car and we drove to the nearest hospital where I registered her.

Little did I know that my modest, spontaneous contribution to the cause of humanity had caught the attention of the local and national media, which gave it considerable prominence. That the only black ambassador in the country had gone to the aid of an injured white Hungarian, who was urgently in need of assistance, whilst her own fellow white citizens had driven off before the arrival of the 'fekete' was a matter of great interest to the people. This tiny act of inter-racial harmony was further reported in the media in Ghana. And to my utter surprise, for a couple of days I had some positive publicity in Ghana, free of charge!

My purpose in narrating these true stories is that racism is evil and repugnant and does a great disservice to mankind, whether perpetrated by white people, as is often the case, or by nonwhite people. When an educated person, who should know better, because of all the immense opportunities that he has received in the world, stoops down to indulge in racism then there is much cause for concern. For whilst the ignorant or uneducated may have a good case for their racist utterances or behavior, the educated, simply does not have a valid reason or excuse for such behavior. Never mind the harm that he is doing unknowingly to his own reputation and the possible career prospects of his children. I am here for the moment excluding any probable legal consequences that may flow from his determination to break the criminal law to satisfy his racist impulses and urges.

The noble and great efforts in 2014/15 by many white nurses, doctors and other volunteers, even at the risk to their own lives, in going to the aid of the millions of West Africans at the risk of infection from the deadly Ebola virus, or dying from it cannot be ignored by any work on racism.

Equally, since 2011, the outstanding and magnanimous action of some European **countries, especially Germany, to offer refuge and safety to millions of people from Syria and parts of North Africa and** the Middle East prove that white people can rise above the inducements and attractions of racism and do the right thing as human beings, even if the skin colour or race of those in utter peril or terrible and dangerous situations is different from theirs. Also the heroic work of thousands of white missionaries, teachers, health workers and volunteers in various parts of South America, Asia, Africa, the Caribbean and the Pacific Region amply demonstrates that the nefarious activities of a tiny minority of active, white racists, aided and abetted sometimes by powerful academics and intellectuals, cannot stop the downward trajectory and imminent demise of the dangerous ideology of racism.

It is my earnest hope that this little work makes a positive contribution to a healthy dialogue on or about racism, leading to its early demise from the world.

I wish to end my book with these famous and profound words by the legendary Dr. Martin Luther King *"I have a dream that my four children will one day live in a nation where they will not be judged by the color of their skin but by the content of their character."* Aug.28, 1963

Finally in case any reader is in any doubt about my long standing stance against racism and my own modest efforts to do something positive to help rid the world of it, I wish to record below these two other personal experiences of mine. For they go to elucidate that nonwhite people who are in a position to do reverse racism can desist from so doing if the will is there. In any case, I do not want to be accused of requesting or pleading with others not to be racist or indulge in racist talk or behavior when I am gleefully doing so myself. For that would be sheer and rant hypocrisy!.

In 1962 whilst I was Ghana ambassador to Hungary and the International Atomic Energy Agency Vienna, Austria, We watched a news item on BBC TV that an English business man by name Grenville Wynne had been arrested and tortured in Budapest, as a spy. Breid and I were in London on vacation. On return to Budapest I was briefed by my Ghanaian staff, who gave me details of what had happened at the Hotel Gellert, where I was in residence for some months till my official residence was ready.

After careful review of the incident I booked an appointment with the Hungarian Foreign Minister. On the morning of the meeting, I put on my best grey suit and for luck, wore my old Achimota College tie. Its striking black and white interwoven stripes appropriately underlined the purpose of my mission. Following a little prayer for Divine help I set off.

After a preliminary brief talk about my stay to date in Hungary I launched politely into a strong protest against the treatment of the alleged spy, Grenville Wynne. And when the kindly Protestant bishop turned statesman/foreign minister said that they had evidence that the man was a spy and that his business as a vendor of caravans was a cover, I replied that if even he was a spy, which I rather doubted, I felt that on purely humanitarian grounds he deserved to be treated better. The minister noted my protest and after amicable and warm handshaking, I left.

As no one from head office in Accra had asked me to intervene as I did, I was putting my high-profile, VIP job on the line by my action. I knew that the alleged spy was white and English and that my action would not earn me any Brownie points in my career. Maybe in Heaven, but not on this planet. I was mindful of the few instances of racism that I had personally suffered in England before going to Hungary, but these negative experiences did not stop me from doing what I felt was the right thing, damn the consequences. For what was at stake was not my little ego but the very life of a fellow human being.

About thirty three years later when Breid and I one night were watching BBC Channel 2 television, I saw and heard with amazement Grenville Wynne, talking of his torture trauma and how it compared with what he went through during his training as a spy. He had some years earlier been released from a Soviet prison in a spy swap between the Soviet Union and the United Kingdom. Then happily living in Spain growing flowers, according to him, he appeared a very friendly and likeable man who had enjoyed life to his satisfaction. Still, notwithstanding his public and gleeful confession in public that he had indeed been a British spy, I am still of the considered opinion that I did the right thing.

In 2009, whilst living in Accra, Ghana, my attention was drawn to a news item in the leading Ghanaian daily newspaper, THE GHANAIN TIMES, whose editor I was several years ago. The story was indeed sad. Two Norwegians, adventurers/businessmen had been condemned to death for allegedly murdering their black driver. They pleaded during the trial that their car had been ambushed by some soldiers who had killed the driver. The long and short of the case was that they were found guilty and sentenced to death. After careful reading of the piece Breid and I decided to do something positive to help the condemned men. So I wrote a strong, pleading letter to the president of the Democratic Republic of the Congo(DCR), H.E.President Joseph Kabila, humbly requesting him to grant clemency to the pair, on humanitarian grounds*. I also drew attention to the noble role that the Scandinavian countries, including Norway, had played in the struggle against apartheid and racism. Although I did not receive a written response to my letter, I was quite happy and satisfied when about two weeks after my letter, a senior diplomat from their embassy in Accra telephoned me and told me that my letter had been received by the 'chef du cabinet', (cabinet secretary) and that it was receiving due attention. I like to feel that my letter plus possibly those from people with great clout contributed towards the decision to commute their sentences to life imprisonment. Sadly, in 2014, we learnt that one of the pair had died in prison. This tragedy should galvanize the need as a matter of urgency to redouble the efforts by all people of goodwill and compassion to help to save Joshua French. The Akan people in Ghana (70 % of the population) have a saying which freely translated says, "The stick with which Kofi was unjustifiably beaten would be used one day against Kwame". In other words, he who witnesses an injustice being perpetrated and does nothing about it may end as a victim of similar injustice.

---

\*

# SOURCES & BIBLIOGRAPHY

I wish to express special gratitude to these sources, which I have found invaluable over the years:

Wikipedia - a great resource

The World Fact Book - Central Intelligence Agency

The Economist: Pocket World In Figures 2014

The BBC

The UN demographic year book

Long Road To Freedom – Nelson Mandela

My American Journey – Gen. Colin Powell

Plus numerous interviews, talks and discussions with a variety of people.

# APPENDIX 1

<u>Important Article In The Journal 'Nature' On Stature & Cognition Characteristics Of the Children Of Mixed Race Marriages & Unions</u>

I take this opportunity to refer readers to an important article in the journal called *Nature* that was published in September 2015. In it, the contributors who are all highly respected scientists from various countries throughout the world have been able to establish after a study of 350,000 people of different races and nationalities that the progeny of mixe race marriages or unions are: **Cleverer and taller than the average**. This article which could easily have been suppressed deserves careful and thorough study by all people of diverse races who wish to understand and contribute to the debate on racism and its implications for the 21ˢᵗ century and the future. Particularly men and women who are involved in race relations work are well advised to study this document. For it goes to show and explain that the cleverness of the Obamas, Kwame Appiahs (Princeton University), Paul Boatengs and others has a scientific and genetic basis. Although this brilliant 12 page highly technical article is long and detailed, it is my hope that an abridged two or three page simplified version can be made available to as wide a public as possible. For it is in the interest of all of us that interracial harmony exists and for this to happen there needs be a good understanding of the genetic basis of the subject.

Furthermore it would be a very good idea if one of the wealthier foundations or universities in America or Europe commissioned a study into the lifespan and health status of a large group similar to the one referred to about. I am convinced on pure anecdotal evidence that the progeny of mixed race unions are not only cleverer and taller but tend to be healthier and live longer than the average. Readers may recall how the English Methodist missionary Rev Thomas B Freeman who was sent from England to the Gold Coast in 1835 as a missionary lived into his 80's at a time when the lifespan on the West African coast for all white traders, adventurers and missionaries was only a matter of few months.

# APPENDIX 2

I think it would be helpful in the understanding of the issues of racism that this historic and important document, the UN charter on Human Rights is reproduced here for careful study by all men and women of good will, especially by those who genuinely wish to see a world rid of racism.

<u>Universal Declaration of Human Rights Preamble</u> Whereas recognition of the inherent dignity and of the equal and inalienable rights of all members of the human family is the foundation of freedom, justice and peace in the world, Whereas disregard and contempt for human rights have resulted in barbarous acts which have outraged the conscience of mankind, and the advent of a world in which human beings shall enjoy freedom of speech and belief and freedom from fear and want has been proclaimed as the highest aspiration of the common people, Whereas it is essential, if man is not to be compelled to have recourse, as a last resort, to rebellion against tyranny and oppression, that human rights should be protected by the rule of law, Whereas it is essential to promote the development of friendly relations between nations, Whereas the peoples of the United Nations have in the Charter reaffirmed their faith in fundamental human rights, in the dignity and worth of the human person and in the equal rights of men and women and have determined to promote social progress and better standards of life in larger freedom, Whereas Member States have pledged themselves to achieve, in cooperation with the United Nations, the promotion of universal respect for and observance of human rights and fundamental freedoms, Whereas a

common understanding of these rights and freedoms is of the greatest importance for the full realization of this pledge, Now, therefore, The General Assembly, Proclaims this Universal Declaration of Human Rights as a common standard of achievement for all peoples and all nations, to the end that every individual and every organ of society, keeping this Declaration constantly in mind, shall strive by teaching and education to promote respect for these rights and freedoms and by progressive measures, national and international, to secure their universal and effective recognition and observance, both among the peoples of Member States themselves and among the peoples of territories under their jurisdiction.

Article I

All human beings are born free and equal in dignity and rights. They are endowed with reason and conscience and should act towards one another in a spirit of brotherhood.

Article 2

Everyone is entitled to all the rights and freedoms set forth in this Declaration, without distinction of any kind, such as race, colour, sex, language, religion, political or other opinion, national or social origin, property, birth or other status. Furthermore, no distinction shall be made on the basis of the political, jurisdictional or international status of the country or territory to which a person belongs, whether it be independent, trust, non-self-governing or under any other limitation of sovereignty.

Article 3

Everyone has the right to life, liberty and security of person.

Article 4

No one shall be held in slavery or servitude; slavery and the slave trade shall be prohibited in all their forms.

Article 5

No one shall be subjected to torture or to cruel, inhuman or degrading treatment or punishment

Article 6

Everyone has the right to recognition everywhere as a person before the law.

Article 7

All are equal before the law and are entitled without any discrimination to equal protection of the law. All are entitled to equal protection against any discrimination in violation of this Declaration and against any incitement to such discrimination.

Article 8

Everyone has the right to an effective remedy by the competent national tribunals for acts violating the fundamental rights granted him by the constitution or by law. Article 9 No one shall be subjected to arbitrary arrest, detention or exile.

Article 10

Everyone is entitled in full equality to a fair and public hearing by an independent and impartial tribunal, in the determination of his rights and obligations and of any criminal charge against him.

Article 11

1. Everyone charged with a penal offence has the right to be presumed innocent until proved guilty according to law in a public trial at which he has had all the guarantees necessary for his defence. 2. No one shall be held guilty of any penal offence on account of any act or omission which did not constitute a penal offence, under national or international law, at the time when it was committed. Nor shall a heavier penalty be imposed than the one that was applicable at the time the penal offence was committed.

Article 12

No one shall be subjected to arbitrary interference with his privacy, family, home or correspondence, nor to attacks upon his honour and reputation. Everyone has the right to the protection of the law against such interference or attacks.

Article 13

1. Everyone has the right to freedom of movement and residence within the borders of each State. 2. Everyone has the right to leave any country, including his own, and to return to his country.

Article 14

1. Everyone has the right to seek and to enjoy in other countries asylum from persecution. 2. This right may not be invoked in the case of prosecutions genuinely arising from non-political crimes or from acts contrary to the purposes and principles of the United Nations.

Article 15

1. Everyone has the right to a nationality. 2. No one shall be arbitrarily deprived of his nationality nor denied the right to change his nationality.

Article 16

1. Men and women of full age, without any limitation due to race, nationality or religion, have the right to marry and to found a family. They are entitled to equal rights as to marriage, during marriage and at its dissolution. 2. Marriage shall be entered into only with the free and full consent of the intending spouses. 3. The family is the natural and fundamental group unit of society and is entitled to protection by society and the State.

Article 17

1. Everyone has the right to own property alone as well as in association with others. 2. No one shall be arbitrarily deprived of his property.

Article 18

Everyone has the right to freedom of thought, conscience and religion; this right includes freedom to change his religion or belief, and freedom, either alone or in community with others and in public or private, to manifest his religion or belief in teaching, practice, worship and observance.

Article 19

Everyone has the right to freedom of opinion and expression; this right includes freedom to hold opinions without interference and to seek, receive and impart information and ideas through any media and regardless of frontiers.

Article 20

1. Everyone has the right to freedom of peaceful assembly and association. 2. No one may be compelled to belong to an association.

Article 21

1. Everyone has the right to take part in the government of his country, directly or through freely chosen representatives. 2. Everyone has the right to equal access to public service in his country. 3. The will of the people shall be the basis of the authority of government; this will shall be expressed in periodic and genuine elections which shall be by universal and equal suffrage and shall be held by secret vote or by equivalent free voting procedures.

Article 22

Everyone, as a member of society, has the right to social security and is entitled to realization, through national effort and international co-operation and in accordance with the organization and resources of each State, of the economic, social and cultural rights indispensable for his dignity and the free development of his personality.

Article 23

1. Everyone has the right to work, to free choice of employment, to just and favourable conditions of work and to protection against unemployment. 2. Everyone, without any discrimination, has the right to equal pay for equal work. 3. Everyone who works has the right to just and favourable remuneration ensuring for himself and his family an existence worthy of human dignity, and supplemented, if necessary, by other means of social protection. 4. Everyone has the right to form and to join trade unions for the protection of his interests.

Article 24

Everyone has the right to rest and leisure, including reasonable limitation of working hours and periodic holidays with pay.

Article 25

1. Everyone has the right to a standard of living adequate for the health and well-being of himself and of his family, including food, clothing, housing and medical care and necessary social services, and the right to security in the event of unemployment, sickness, disability, widowhood, old age or other lack of livelihood in circumstances beyond his control. 2. Motherhood and childhood are

entitled to special care and assistance. All children, whether born in or out of wedlock, shall enjoy the same social protection.

Article 26

1. Everyone has the right to education. Education shall be free, at least in the elementary and fundamental stages. Elementary education shall be compulsory. Technical and professional education shall be made generally available and higher education shall be equally accessible to all on the basis of merit. 2. Education shall be directed to the full development of the human personality and to the strengthening of respect for human rights and fundamental freedoms. It shall promote understanding, tolerance and friendship among all nations, racial or religious groups, and shall further the activities of the United Nations for the maintenance of peace. 3. Parents have a prior right to choose the kind of education that shall be given to their children.

Article 27

1. Everyone has the right freely to participate in the cultural life of the community, to enjoy the arts and to share in scientific advancement and its benefits. 2. Everyone has the right to the protection of the moral and material interests resulting from any scientific, literary or artistic production of which he is the author.

Article 28

Everyone is entitled to a social and international order in which the rights and freedoms set forth in this Declaration can be fully realized.

Article 29

1. Everyone has duties to the community in which alone the free and full development of his personality is possible. 2. In the exercise of his rights and freedoms, everyone shall be subject only to such limitations as are determined by law solely for the purpose of securing due recognition and respect for the rights and freedoms of others and of meeting the just requirements of morality, public order and the general welfare in a democratic society. 3. These rights and freedoms may in no case be exercised contrary to the purposes and principles of the United Nations.

Article 30

Nothing in this Declaration may be interpreted as implying for any State, group or person any right to engage in any activity or to perform any act aimed at the destruction of any of the rights and freedoms set forth herein.

# APPENDIX 3

*Another very important document on racism, that needs thorough study, by all people involved in the campaigns or programmes against racism, to carefully consider is reproduced here in parts.*

World Conference against Racism, Racial Discrimination, Xenophobia and Related Intolerance Declaration Having met in Durban, South Africa, from 31 August to 8 September 2001, Expressing deep appreciation to the Government of South Africa for hosting this World Conference, Drawing inspiration from the heroic struggle of the people of South Africa against the institutionalized system of apartheid, as well as for equality and justice under democracy, development, the rule of law and respect for human rights, recalling in this context the important contribution to that struggle of the international community and, in particular, the pivotal role of the people and Governments of Africa, and noting the important role that different actors of civil society, including non-governmental organizations, played in that struggle and in ongoing efforts to combat racism, racial discrimination, xenophobia and related intolerance, Recalling that the Vienna Declaration and Programme of Action, adopted by the World Conference on Human Rights in June 1993, calls for the speedy and comprehensive elimination of all forms of racism, racial discrimination, xenophobia and related intolerance, Recalling Commission on Human Rights resolution 1997/74 of 18 April 1997, General Assembly resolution 52/111 of 12 December 1997 and subsequent resolutions of those bodies concerning the convening of the World Conference against Racism, Racial Discrimination, Xenophobia and Related Intolerance and recalling also the two World Conferences to Combat Racism and Racial Discrimination, held in Geneva in 1978 and 1983, respectively, Noting with grave concern that despite the efforts of the international community, the principal objectives of the three Decades to Combat Racism and Racial Discrimination have not been attained and that countless human beings continue to the present day to be victims of racism, racial discrimination, xenophobia and related intolerance, Recalling that the year 2001 is the International Year of Mobilization against Racism, Racial Discrimination, Xenophobia and Related Intolerance, aimed at drawing the world's attention to the objectives of the World Conference and giving new momentum to the political commitment to eliminate all forms of racism, racial discrimination, xenophobia and related intolerance, Welcoming the decision of the General Assembly to proclaim the year 2001 as the United Nations Year of Dialogue among Civilizations, which underlines tolerance and respect for diversity and the need to seek common ground among and within civilizations in order to address common challenges to humanity that threaten shared values, universal human rights and the fight against racism, racial discrimination, xenophobia and related intolerance, through cooperation, partnership and inclusion, - 2 - Welcoming also the proclamation by the General Assembly of the period 2001-2010 as the Decade for a Culture of Peace and Non-Violence for Children of the World, as well as the adoption by the General Assembly of the Declaration and Plan of Action on a Culture of Peace, Recognizing that the World Conference against Racism, Racial Discrimination, Xenophobia and Related Intolerance, in conjunction with the International Decade of the World's Indigenous People, presents a unique opportunity to consider the invaluable contributions of indigenous peoples to political, economic, social, cultural and spiritual development throughout the world to our societies, as well as the challenges faced by them, including racism and racial discrimination, Recalling the United Nations Declaration on the Granting of Independence to Colonial

Countries and Peoples of 1960, Reaffirming our commitment to the purposes and principles contained in the Charter of the United Nations and the Universal Declaration of Human Rights, Affirming that racism, racial discrimination, xenophobia and related intolerance constitute a negation of the purposes and principles of the Charter of the United Nations, Reaffirming the principles of equality and non-discrimination in the Universal Declaration of Human Rights and encouraging respect for human rights and fundamental freedoms for all without distinction of any kind such as race, colour, sex, language, religion, political or other opinion, national or social origin, property, birth or other status, Convinced of the fundamental importance of universal accession to or ratification of and full implementation of our obligations arising under the International Convention on the Elimination of All Forms of Racial Discrimination as the principal international instrument to eliminate racism, racial discrimination, xenophobia and related intolerance, Recognizing the fundamental importance for States, in combating racism, racial discrimination, xenophobia, and related intolerance, to consider signing, ratifying or acceding to all relevant international human rights instruments, with a view to universal adherence, Having taken note of the reports of the regional conferences organized at Strasbourg, Santiago, Dakar and Tehran and other inputs from States, as well as the reports of expert seminars, non-governmental organization regional meetings and other meetings organized in preparation for the World Conference, Noting with appreciation the Vision Statement launched by President Thabo Mbeki of South Africa under the patronage of The Honourable Nelson Mandela, first President of the new South Africa, and at the initiative of the United Nations High Commissioner for Human Rights and Secretary-General of the World Conference, and signed by seventy-four heads of State, heads of Government and dignitaries.

Civil society 210. Calls upon States to strengthen cooperation, develop partnerships and consult regularly with non-governmental organizations and all other sectors of the civil society to harness their experience and expertise, thereby contributing to the development of legislation, policies and other governmental initiatives, as well as involving them more closely in the elaboration and implementation of policies and programmes designed to combat racism, racial discrimination, xenophobia and related intolerance; 211. Urges leaders of religious communities to continue to confront racism, racial discrimination, xenophobia and related intolerance through, inter alia, promotion and sponsoring of dialogue and partnerships to bring about reconciliation, healing and harmony within and among societies, invites religious communities to participate in promoting economic and social revitalization and encourages religious leaders to foster greater cooperation and contact between diverse racial groups; 212. Urges States to establish and strengthen effective partnerships with and provide support, as appropriate, to all relevant actors of civil society, including non-governmental organizations working to promote gender equality and the advancement of women, particularly women subject to multiple discrimination, and to promote an integrated and holistic approach to the elimination of all forms of discrimination against women and girls; Non-governmental organizations 213. Urges States to provide an open and conducive environment to enable non-governmental organizations to function freely and openly within their societies and thereby make an effective contribution to the elimination of racism, racial discrimination, xenophobia and related intolerance throughout the world, and to promote a wider role for grass-roots organizations; 214. Calls upon States to explore means to expand the role of non-governmental organizations in society through, in particular, deepening the ties of solidarity amongst citizens and promoting greater trust across racial and social class divides by promoting wider citizen involvement and more voluntary cooperation; The private sector 215. Urges States to take measures, including, where appropriate, legislative measures, to ensure that transnational corporations and other foreign enterprises operating within their national territories conform to precepts and practices of non-racism and non-discrimination, and further encourages the business sector, including transnational corporations and foreign enterprises, to collaborate with trade unions and other relevant sectors of civil society to develop - 61 - voluntary codes of conduct for all businesses, designed to prevent, address and eradicate racism, racial discrimination, xenophobia and related intolerance; Youth 216. Urges States to encourage the full and active participation of, as well as involve more closely, youth in the elaboration, planning and implementation of activities to fight racism, racial discrimination, xenophobia and related intolerance, and calls upon States, in partnership with non-governmental organizations and other sectors of society, to facilitate both national and international youth dialogue on racism, racial discrimination, xenophobia and related intolerance, through the World Youth Forum of the United Nations system and through the use of new technologies, exchanges and other means; 217. Urges States to encourage and facilitate the establishment and maintenance of youth mechanisms, set up by youth organizations and young women and men themselves, in the spirit of combating racism, racial discrimination, xenophobia and related intolerance, through such activities as: disseminating and exchanging information and building networks to these ends; organizing awareness-raising campaigns and participating in multicultural education programmes; developing proposals and solutions, where possible and appropriate; cooperating and consulting regularly with non-governmental organizations and other actors in civil society in developing initiatives and programmes that promote intercultural exchange and dialogue; 218. Urges States, in cooperation with intergovernmental organizations, the International Olympic Committee and international and regional sports federations, to intensify the fight against racism in sport by, among other things, educating the youth of the world through sport practised without discrimination of any kind and in the Olympic spirit, which requires human understanding, tolerance, fair play and solidarity; 219. Recognizes that the success of this Programme of Action will require political will and adequate funding at the national, regional and international levels, and international cooperation. Notes 1 For the purpose of this Declaration and Programme of Action, it was understood that the term "gender" refers to the two sexes, male and female, within the context of society. The term "gender" does not indicate any meaning different from the above. 2 Reference should be made to chapter VII of the report of the Conference, which lists all the reservations to and statements on the Declaration and the Programme of Action.

# APPENDIX 4

**Dialogue With The Reader**

1) As a reader, are you of the view that the writer has made a compelling case for good interracial relations?

2) Do you accept the view put forward by the writer that white women are not racist or at worst are insignificantly so compared with the men?

3) Can racism be eradicated or is it destined to plague the world for more centuries to come?

4) If bi-racial marriages and unions contribute towards elimination of racism ala Enoch Powell, then should governments consider launching programmes to encourage and advance interracial marriages and unions as these have been established to produce cleverer and taller people?

5) Are people born racist in other words is it a genetic characteristic or is it acquired and not inheritable?

6) Is it likely that if racism is not eradicated as soon as possible in a few decades to come the world might witness reverse racism namely non-white people discriminating against white people?

7) Do you share the author's view that people should only be accepted into race relations work who have shown by their proven track record either as volunteers or by marriage or

by specific actions or statements that they are genuinely committed to contributing to the eradication of racism?

Your views and comments will be most welcome with much gratitude.

- Joseph Godson Amamoo
  (kwaws100@gmail.com)

# APPENDIX 5

Other Books by the Author, Also known as the sons of the Author

**THE NEW GHANA**

**CONSTITUTIONAL PROPOSALS FOR POST – COUP AFRICA**

**THE GHANAIAN REVOLUTION**

**THE CHOCOLATE LADY (novel)**

**THE QUEEN's MEN (novel)**

**THE AFRICAN PRINCESS (novel)**

**THE AMBASSADOR (novel)**

**GHANA – 50 YEARS OF INDEPENDENCE**

**GOD's HAND AT WORK**

**MY AFRICAN JOURNEY (Autobiography)**

**AFRICA – RICH BUT POOR**

Printed in the United States
By Bookmasters